KV-372-906

HOW TO DO
WELL
IN MUSIC EXAMS

A guide for students, parents and
teachers to the Graded Music Examinations
of the Associated Board of the Royal
Schools of Music, Guildhall School of
Music and Drama, Trinity College of
Music and London College of Music

Rudolph Sabor

ANDRE DEUTSCH

First published in Great Britain 1989
by André Deutsch Limited
105–106 Great Russell Street London WC1

British Library Cataloguing in Publication Data

Sabor, Rudolph
How to do well in music exams.
1. Musical instrument playing
I. Title
780′.1

ISBN 0-233-98387-2 (hardback edition)
ISBN 0-233-98463-1 (paperback edition)

Copyright © 1989 by Rudolph Sabor
All rights reserved

Printed in Great Britain by
Billing and Sons Ltd, Worcester

HOW TO DO WELL IN MUSIC EXAMS

By the same author

THE REAL WAGNER

For Emmi, Monika and Peter

CONTENTS

Acknowledgements

My thanks to my helpers.

Monika and Peter Sabor have monitored and fostered the script with a loving but merciless eye. Without them, the book could not have been written.

Larry Adler, Norbert Brainin, Sir Colin Davis, Bryan Fairfax, Robert Farley, James Galway, Antony Hopkins, Peter Katin, Julian Lloyd Webber, Moura Lympani, Peter Wallfisch and Hilary Williams have all yielded to the author's entreaties for morsels from their tables. In their generosity they sent whole loaves.

I am indebted to a number of outstanding teachers for their advice and encouragement. They are: Mike Bailey, Keith Banner, Wendy Cox, Malcolm Fletcher, Robert Henty, Emmi Sabor.

A medley of music students between five and eighty-three enriched this book with their views. May they flourish.

Introduction

Within the next twenty-four months one million English-speaking students – very young, young, middle-aged, old and very old – will have taken a graded music examination. The route to success is a circuitous one, with a fair number of casualties littering the roadside. *How To Do Well in Music Exams* presents and clarifies the entire process, from choosing the right instrument and avoiding the wrong teacher to striding from the examination room with a victor's smile.

Written in practical terms by a former examiner, the book addresses students of all ages, their families and their teachers. Its aim is to turn failures into passes, passes into credits, credits into distinctions, and the whole process into a journey to the promised land of music.

Lists of 'Suggested Study' and 'Suggested Listening' are intended to help expand the student's view of his or her instrument, and the reader will also find information on the whereabouts of professional organizations, sources of advice and help, music shops, etc. The information about addresses and telephone numbers, costs of new and second-hand instruments, and tuition fees, must inevitably begin to date from the moment of publication, but it has seemed worth while to collect it between one pair of covers, and readers will be able to make their own judgement about percentages to be added to allow for inflation and other price shifts.

Fact File I offers a brief view of the new GCSE Music exam, and other Fact Files list the principal music retailers, interpret the forest of initials after teachers' names which denote their degrees and diplomas, and give the phone numbers to call for musical assistance in as many parts of the United Kingdom as the author has been able to document.

As your instrumental or vocal or theoretical skill increases – and increase it will – you may wish for an independent assessment of your present achievement, together with expert advice on how to improve. In other words, you will take an examination in music.

There are several establishments which offer music examinations, ranging from 'Preliminary' to 'Grade 8'. Beyond that, there are diplomas and degrees to be gained, but these are outside the scope of this book. The following Table familiarizes you with the available options. *Yes* means you can take that particular examination with that particular examination board. *No* means you cannot. Here and elsewhere, these abbreviations have been used:

AB   Associated Board of the Royal Schools of Music.
G   Guildhall School of Music and Drama.
T   Trinity College of Music, London.
L   London College of Music.

	AB	G	T	L
Piano	Yes	Yes	Yes	Yes
Piano Duet	Yes	No	Yes	No
Harpsichord	Yes	No	Yes	No
Organ	Yes	No	Yes	Yes
Electronic Organ	No	Yes	Yes	Yes
Violin	Yes	Yes	Yes	Yes
Viola	Yes	Yes	Yes	Yes
Violoncello	Yes	Yes	Yes	Yes
Double Bass	Yes	No	Yes	Yes
Guitar	Yes	Yes	Yes	Yes
Guitar Duet	No	No	Yes	No
Harp	Yes	No	Yes	No
Singing	Yes	Yes	Yes	Yes
Recorder	Yes	Yes	Yes	Yes
Flute	Yes	Yes	Yes	Yes
Oboe	Yes	Yes	Yes	Yes
Clarinet	Yes	Yes	Yes	Yes
Bassoon	Yes	Yes	Yes	Yes
Saxophone	Yes	Yes	Yes	Yes
French Horn	Yes	Yes	Yes	Yes
Trumpet	Yes	Yes	Yes	Yes
Cornet	Yes	Yes	Yes	Yes
Trombone	Yes	Yes	Yes	Yes
Tuba	Yes	Yes	Yes	No
Flugelhorn	Yes	Yes	Yes	No
E Flat Horn	Yes	Yes	Yes	No
Baritone	Yes	Yes	Yes	No
Euphonium	Yes	Yes	Yes	No
E Flat Bass	Yes	Yes	Yes	No
B Flat Bass	Yes	Yes	Yes	No
Percussion	No	Yes	Yes	No

Practical Musicianship	Yes	Yes	Yes	No
Theory	Yes	Yes	Yes	Yes

You will of course keep abreast of any alterations to the above Table, by obtaining Regulations and Subject Syllabuses from the Examination Boards, as required:

Associated Board of the Royal Schools of Music
14 Bedford Square, London WC1B 3JG
Tel.: 01 636 4478

Guildhall School of Music and Drama
Barbican, Silk Street, London EC2Y 8DT
Tel.: 01 628 2571

Trinity College of Music
11 Mandeville Place, London W1M 6AQ
Tel.: 01 935 5773

London College of Music
47 Great Marlborough Street, London W1V 2AS
Tel.: 01 437 6120

1 CHOOSING YOUR INSTRUMENT

This chapter surveys the scene.

You, the prospective examination candidate, have either already started on your path, or you are contemplating doing so. In either case, the following will be of immediate concern to you.

To stir the keys of your piano into life, to guide your bow across responsive strings, to coax melodies out of a hollow tube, to make coiled metal answer with a whole range of sound from whisper to shriek, to wield the timpani sticks that make you lord of timing and time – those are the joys and achievements that may be yours for life.

Not that they are easily won. But you are not alone. *You are part of a team.* You are the captain, and your teacher, your parents, your school, your friends and your examiner are your supporters. So is this book and – most important – so is your chosen instrument. Together you will be setting out on a journey of discovery. You will conquer all hazards, you will enjoy your growing skill, day by day, week by week, month by month.

Matchmaking

Before deciding on the instrument of your choice, eliminate the unsuitable ones. This will save time, expense and frustration. Unsuitable? Imagine a short, wiry person wrestling with a Euphonium or a Double Bass. Player and instrument should match each other. Your own physical and mental characteristics should not contradict those of your musical instrument. Peruse this list and cross off those instruments which are likely to disagree with you, but remember that handicaps can be overcome.

Because I	I shall avoid	But I will consider
am slightly built	Viola Cello Double Bass Bassoon Trombone Euphonium	Piano Violin Guitar Recorder Cornet E Flat Horn
have breathing problems	Oboe French Horn Trumpet Trombone Tuba Euphonium	almost everything else
have pitch problems	Violin Viola Cello Double Bass Bassoon Trombone	Piano Guitar Percussion (but not Timpani)
have poor eyesight	Piano Organ	everything else
have short arms	Viola Double Bass Flute Trombone Tuba	everything else
have small hands	Viola Cello Double Bass Bassoon	Violin Recorder Oboe Clarinet Trumpet Cornet E Flat Horn Percussion
have slender finger tips	Clarinet Bassoon	almost everything else

Because I	I shall avoid	But I will consider
am left-handed	Flute	Piano Violin Viola Cello Double Bass Guitar French Horn Trombone
have rather thin lips	Saxophone Trombone	Oboe and almost everything else
have rather thick lips	Flute Oboe French Horn	everything else
have small front teeth	Saxophone	everything else
have strong front teeth	Flute	Clarinet and everything else

wear dentures/a
  brace/have not
  very good teeth
	Brass Instrs	almost everything else

still have my first teeth	Trumpet Cornet	everything else, age allowing

am a splendid
  person, but mental
  agility is not my
  strongest point
	Piano
	Organ
	Double Bass
	Guitar
	Harp
	Saxophone
	French Horn
	Trumpet
	Trombone
		everything else

am prone to dizzy spells	Flute Oboe Trumpet Trombone Tuba	everything else

Because I	I shall avoid	But I will consider
like quick results	Violin Oboe Bassoon French Horn	Clarinet Saxophone E Flat Horn Baritone
am a loner	Double Bass Bassoon	Piano Organ Guitar French Horn
must not make much noise (Flat – neighbours – night shift etc)	Trumpet Drums Electric Guitar	Cello Guitar Harp Euphonium
have restricted means	Oboe Bassoon Saxophone French Horn Tuba Harp	Violin Guitar Recorder Clarinet Trumpet Cornet E Flat Horn
have little spare space/no ready transport	Double Bass Harp Tuba	Violin Viola Guitar Recorder Flute Oboe Clarinet Trumpet Cornet E Flat Horn Baritone

While you are about it, delete also those instruments for which no teacher can be found (see next chapter), and those for which you are too young:

Possible starting age

Years	Instrument
3	Violin
5	Recorder – Piano
6	Guitar
9	Cello – Cornet
10	Clarinet – E Flat Horn
11	Viola – Flute – Saxophone – Trumpet
12	Oboe – French Horn – Trombone – Baritone
13	Harp – Organ – Euphonium
14	Bassoon
15	Double Bass – Tuba – E Flat Bass – B Flat Bass

You have drawn up a short list of likely instruments. Let us assume you are interested in Piano, Violin, Flute and Trumpet. You will of course have seen and listened to a pianist in action. But have you had a chance to observe a violinist, a flautist, a trumpeter? You can watch them in school ensembles, in local amateur orchestras, in the concert hall, on television. Familiarize yourself with the sounds they produce. Obtain tapes, records or compact discs from your public library of, say:

A Schubert Piano Sonata;
Beethoven's Violin Concerto;
James Galway playing anything on his Flute;
Shostakovich's Trumpet Concerto.

Four totally different experiences in sound. Listen critically. Which *sound* – not necessarily which *music* – appeals to you most? Could you live with it for years to come? Fact File II lists addresses and phone numbers of a selection of instrument manufacturers and retailers in Great Britain and Northern Ireland.

The following survey contains notes on all listed instruments, with brief descriptions of how they work, pointing out snags as well as benefits, listing important music, and suggesting ways of purchasing, hiring, borrowing or gaining access.

5

Piano

* Popularity Rating: 1/16

The Pianoforte is the most important of all musical instruments: its invention was to music what the invention of printing was to poetry.
GEORGE BERNARD SHAW

When you depress the keys, white or black, felt-covered wooden hammers inside the instrument strike the strings. The high strings, to the right of the player, are thinner and shorter than the low strings, to the left of the player. As soon as you allow the keys to return to their position of rest, a damper action causes the sound to stop. You do not have to search for the correct pitch, as on so many other instruments. It is ready made for you. This is pleasant for students with pitch problems, but it should not prevent you from seeking to improve your aural perception. You will have to pass a set of aural tests for your music examinations. More important, a keen ear helps you to get much more out of music, your own and other people's, than an indifferent one. Chapter 3 shows you how to increase your listening powers.

The Piano has this advantage over all other instruments: there are so many more teachers. Also, the literature (i.e. music written for the instrument) is immense and readily available. Quite apart from studying your technique and your current pieces, you can 'browse', playing melodies (right hand) of songs, investigating bass lines (left hand) of concertos and symphonies, dipping into any section of music you fancy, lingering here, skipping there – in short, browsing will do wonders for your sight reading, apart from introducing you to the music of the ages. A proficient sight reader will be in demand, helping other instrumentalists and, in his own right, in groups and bands.

The keyboard instrument is unique: it commands both melody and harmony. Thus you can create your own self-contained world of sound, by playing the scores of orchestral and chamber works, as well as operas, oratorios and ballets.

As a pianist, you will be able to grasp the rudiments and theory of music with comparative ease. But you will have to cope with reading two staves and two clefs, one for each hand; with using both feet, one for each pedal; and your eyes will have to get used to changing their focus

---

* Popularity Rating: based on a survey of entries to practical examinations in keyboard and orchestral instruments and singing. Example: Piano 1/16 = out of sixteen examination subjects, averaged over all grades, the Piano was the most popular one.

frequently, as they scan the printed music and keep ten fingers under observation, in rapid and constant succession. Coping with two staves and clefs at a time sounds more terrifying than it is. Consider the conductor of a symphony orchestra who has to read sixteen, twenty or more staves simultaneously, with more than two clefs at a time. Lucky pianist!

The Piano can be started at a very early age, or indeed at any time of life. Many elderly people find studying the Piano to be fulfilling and rewarding.

It is often assumed that the Piano is a solitary instrument. It is, in fact, as solitary or as gregarious as you choose to make it. You can immerse yourself, in splendid isolation, in Chopin's nocturnal world, or you can partner a friend in a duet for four hands, or two friends in a trio for six hands. Where there are two pianos together, up to six players can revel in rare romps with their twelve hands or sixty fingers. You can accompany a violinist, a flautist, a trumpeter, a singer, a vocal group, a full choir, and even dancers. With growing skill, you might be able to discover the wonders of chamber music, playing in a piano trio (Piano, Violin and Cello), in a piano quartet or quintet. School orchestras frequently need a pianist, to support weaker players or to fill in the parts of missing ones. As a pianist, you need never be alone.

The time may come when you wish to spread your wings and take up a second instrument. Many successful transitions have been made from the Piano to the Organ, the Guitar, the Double Bass, the Timpani, the Xylophone and, of course, the Harpsichord. It may be a little late, after several years as a pianist, to make a start on the Violin, Viola or Cello, but Clarinet, Trumpet, Trombone, Tuba and other non-orchestral brass instruments are feasible candidates, not forgetting the voice and such examination subjects as Theory and General Musicianship.

The next chapter discusses the all-important topic of how to find a suitable teacher. For now we shall consider how to obtain an adequate instrument. Beware the one that is advertised as 'suitable for a beginner', whether Piano, Clarinet, Guitar or anything else. It usually means, 'this is a nasty, clapped-out piece of junk, but who are you to notice, being a mere beginner?' The beginner's instrument must be a quality instrument, or progress will be slow, a faulty technique may be acquired and the beginner and his listeners will lose heart. This is where your team springs into action. Ask your friends, your school music teacher, members of your family to locate that ugly duckling piano in someone's attic, in a second-hand furniture shop, at your or your team's local piano store, and have it checked over. It may turn out to be a swan. Who is to do the checking? An expert of course. There is no greater expert than the skilled piano tuner. Find one by asking your school music teacher, or look in the yellow pages. If the tuner has one of these sets of initials after his name – ABPT, MPTA, MIMIT – you may assume that he knows his job. They stand for:

Association of Blind Piano Tuners, 24 Fairlawn Grove, London W4 5EH
Member of the Pianoforte Tuners Association, 5 Northdown, Ashford, Kent TN24 8RB
Member of the Institute of Musical Instrument Technology, 134 Crouch Hill, London N8 9DX

Tell him you are likely to ask him to tune your Piano in future, and he will think twice before recommending an instrument which will cause him trouble for the rest of his or its life.

A newcomer to the second-hand scene is a firm which describes itself as 'the nationwide computerized buying and selling agency of musical instruments and accessories'. Obtain details from Databoard, 75 London St, Farringdon, Oxon SN7 7AG.

An interesting range of services is provided by The Piano Workshop, 30A Highgate Rd, London NW5 1NS. They sell new and restored instruments, operate rental and credit schemes, offer part-exchange facilities, and provide tuning, restoration and valuation services.

You will not get much of a second-hand Piano for under £1000. Here are some typical current prices:

Restored Uprights

Kemble	£990
Chappell	£1330
Rogers	£1495
Broadwood	£1725
Welmar	£2595
Bechstein	£3625

Restored Grands

Collard	£1995
Brinsmead	£3250
Bechstein	£5500

New Uprights

Young Chang (S. Korea)	from £1350
Fazer (Finland)	from £1515
Knight (Britain)	from £2190

| Welmar (Britain) | from £2575 |
| Blüthner (E. Germany) | from £4800 |

New Grands

Young Chang	from £3690
Zimmermann (E. Germany)	from £4000
Blüthner	from £9400

The wisdom of *hiring* a Piano may appeal to you. Your local piano or music shop will put you in touch with firms that run such a scheme. Go for one that offers 'option to purchase'. You hire for three months or longer. During that period you will decide, first whether the Piano as such appeals to you, and second whether you like the hired instrument. If you then wish to buy it, your hire fee will be deducted from the purchase price. On the whole, this seems to be the most sensible way of procuring a Piano or, for that matter, any other musical instrument. But don't forget to ask your expert to vet it first.

You have now found your Piano. *Will it get into your home?* Are there stairs or awkward turnings to be negotiated? Discuss this with your movers, before they are forced to call for a crane and have it dropped through the roof.

Whatever location you have in mind for your new friend, don't invite him into your bedroom. Pianos loathe changes of temperature. They object to being placed near a radiator. They take a dim view of basements. They sniff at damp outer walls. So find a cosy position where there are no wild fluctuations of temperature, and put a few potted plants in its vicinity, to act as humidifiers. For an added treat, place a shallow jug or two filled with water inside its bottom front panel, and hang a few mothballs near its felt-covered hammers (the top front panel is as easily detachable as the lower one).

If you can afford a new Piano, in addition to the traditional English and German sounds the exciting range of East Asian instruments should be looked at. They are well made, good to handle, pleasantly responsive, and they sound rather beautiful. Contact these and other reliable manufacturers:

Bentley Pianos, Woodchester Mills, Stroud, Glos, GL5 5NW
Blüthner Pianos, 47 Conduit St, London WIR ODS
Bösendorfer Pianos, 38 Wigmore St, London W1H 9DF
Brinsmead and Chappell Pianos, Mount Ave, Bletchley, Milton Keynes MK1 1JE
Broadwood Pianos, 45a High St, Stony Stratford, Milton Keynes MK11 1AA

Kawai Pianos, 94 Jermyn St, London SW1

Knight Pianos, Langston Rd, Debden Ind. Estate, Loughton, Essex 1G10 3TL

Monington & Weston, 13 Brecknock Rd, London N7 OBL

Robert Morley, 4 Belmont Hill, London SE13 5BD

Samuel Pianos, 142 Edgware Rd, London W2 2DZ

Schimmel Pianos, 126 Deansgate, Manchester M3 2GR

Steinway & Sons, 44 Marylebone Lane, London W1M 6EN

Whelpdale, Maxwell & Codd, 47 Conduit St, London W1R ODS

Yamaha-Kemble Pianos, Mount Ave, Bletchley, Milton Keynes, MK1 1JE

Young Chang Pianos, 30a Highgate Rd, London NW5 1NS

The number of instruction manuals for the Piano, as well as for all other instruments, for the Voice, for Theory and for General Musicianship is practically limitless. The ones listed below constitute a selection of useful publications which, by its nature, cannot pretend to include everything that ought to be included. Parents and other team members of prospective students of the Piano, or of any other examination subject listed further on, may wish to inspect one or the other Tutor, in order to acquaint themselves, superficially at least, with the requirements peculiar to the chosen instrument or other examination subject.

All items listed under 'Study' can be obtained either through your local music shop or from a firm dealing with all or many music publishers. Addresses of such firms will be found in the *British Music Yearbook* (look in your Public Library), under 'Directory: Trade'. Here are just a few, for your guidance:

Blackwell's, 38 Holywell St, Oxford OX1 3SW

Chappell, 50 New Bond St, London W1Y 9HA

Cramer, 23 Garrick St, London WC2E 9AX

Educational Music Services, 22 Mountjoy Sq., Dublin

Elkin, Station Rd, Ind. Estate, Salhouse, Norwich NR13 6NY

Forsyth, Gt George St, Leeds LS1 3DL

Minns, 158 Above Bar, Southampton SO1 ODU

Ron's Music Shop, Ilford Lane, Ilford, Essex IG1 2RD

Stamford Music Shop, 11 St Mary's, Stamford, Lincs PE9 2DP

SUGGESTED STUDY

Piano Tutors: Young Beginners

Barratt: *Chester's Piano Book* (Chester)
Bowen: *The Simplicity of Piano Technique* (Stainer & Bell)
Ching: *Piano Primer* (Chappell)
Cooke: *Tone, Touch and Technique for the Young Pianist* (Allans)
Grindea: *The First Ten Lessons* (OUP)
Harrison: *The Young Person's Guide To Playing the Piano* (Faber)
Last: *At the Keyboard* (OUP)
Peanuts Piano Course (Boosey & Hawkes)
Russian School of Piano Playing (Boosey & Hawkes)
Teggin: *Pianosounds* (Boosey & Hawkes)
Waterman & Harewood: *Piano Lessons* (Faber)
Waterman & Harewood: *Piano Playtime* (Faber)

Piano Tutors: Adult Beginners
Aaron: *Adult Piano Course* (Belwin Mills)
Baker: *The Complete Piano Player* (Wise)
Bastien: *The Older Beginner Piano Course* (Fentone)
Glover: *Adult Piano Student* (Belwin Mills)
Harrison: *Adult Piano Tutor* (Faber)
Kirkby-Mason: *The Adult Beginner* (Bosworth)
Noona: *The Adult Pianist* (Heritage)
Schaum: *Adult Piano Course* (Cramer)

Jazz
Jazz Solal (Boosey & Hawkes)
King: *Progressive Jazz for Juniors* (Kalmus)
Norton: *Microjazz for Starters* (Boosey & Hawkes)

SUGGESTED LISTENING
Beethoven: Sonatas and Concertos
Mozart: Sonatas and Concertos
Schubert: Sonatas
Bach: Preludes and Fugues
Brahms: Intermezzos
Debussy: *Children's Corner* Suite
Grieg: Piano Concerto
Chopin: Waltzes, Mazurkas, Polonaises
Saint-Saëns: *Carnival of the Animals*

Jazz piano: Bill Evans, Herbie Hancock, Keith Jarrett, Thelonius Monk, Oscar Peterson

POSTSCRIPT

'Dear Colleague, I occasionally find that we have old pianos which are beyond repair. It may be that . . . these could be used within your music departments. I should be grateful if you would indicate if you may be interested in having such an old instrument redirected to your school.'

Letter to all heads of music in secondary
schools in Avon from senior music adviser
(from the *Times Educational Supplement*, 19.6.1987).

Harpsichord

Popularity rating: unavailable

It was Mr Western's custom every afternoon, as soon as he was drunk, to hear his daughter play on the harpsichord; for he was a great lover of music.

HENRY FIELDING, *Tom Jones*

The harpsichordist of bygone ages was a skilled craftsman. In addition to playing the written notes, he had to add copious ornaments, in the style of the period, and he was required to supply the harmonies which the composer only indicated without troubling to write them out. He would also be expected to be able to extemporize – i.e. play music of his own invention, in the manner of the piece being performed – where the composer wished this to be done. In the nineteenth century the Harpsichord lost its popularity and virtually disappeared. A musical world which delighted in listening to oratorios in the Albert Hall, performed by colossal choirs of a thousand voices, and orchestral forces to match, found little merit in the still, intense, beautiful voice of the Harpsichord. Today, however, the instrument has staged a dramatic comeback. Dozens of manufacturers are hardly able to keep up with the demand, and some interesting new music has been written for the Harpsichord of our time.

You play the Harpsichord by operating a piano-like keyboard. But the similarity ends there. When you depress a key, the strings are not struck, as on the Piano, but *plucked* by means of a plectrum made of quill, leather or synthetic material. This plectrum is fixed to a wooden 'jack' which is stirred into motion as your fingers activate the keys. Timbre and, to a certain extent, volume of tone can be varied by means of stops (as on the

12

Organ) or pedals (as on the Piano). There are one, two or even three keyboards, but the tone of the Harpsichord is far quieter than that of the Piano – advantageous for unappreciative neighbours, but tricky in concert halls, where it frequently requires amplification.

The Harpsichord needs a great deal of tuning and even re-tuning during concerts, and the prospective player will have to learn how to perform this essential service. One or two remarkable tuning devices have recently appeared which make this less of a chore. Your supplier will be able to give you details.

If you wish to become a harpsichordist, you will have had several years experience on the Piano; you will have fallen in love with the unique silver sound of the instrument; you will be prepared to learn the tuning process; you will like the idea of studying 'figured bass'. For the latter purpose invest in:

Morris: *Figured Harmony at the Keyboard* (Oxford University Press).

You will also have to establish access to an instrument and secure a course of consultation lessons with a *specialist* teacher (see chapter 2). Your progress can be monitored and encouraged by the graded examinations held by the Associated Board and Trinity College of Music. Expert advice is available for the asking. Contact:

Early Music Centre, Information Service,
Charles Clore House, 17 Russell Square,
London WC1B 5DR (01-580-8401)

HARPSICHORD MAKERS
Here is a selection of addresses. Some may be able to offer hire schemes and/or provide complete kits for home assembly:

D. H. Bolton, 17 The Crescent, Linthorpe, Middlesbrough, Cleveland TS5 6SG
Michael Cole, Little Tatchley, 334 Prestbury Rd, Cheltenham, Glos GL52 3DD
Hugh Craig, The Nupend, Cradley, Worcs WR13 5NP
Robert Deegan, Tonnage Warehouse, St George's Quay, Lancaster LA1 1RB
J. & M. Dolmetsch, 107–108 Blackdown Rural Industries, Haste Hill, Haslemere, Surrey GU27 3AY
Clive Dunkley, Millfield, Cobham Rd, Stoke d'Abernon, Cobham, Surrey KT11 3QQ

Robert Goble, Greatstones, Kiln Lane, Headington, Oxford OX3 8HQ
Alan Gotto, 5 Bessemer Rd, Norwich NR4 4DQ
Michael Heale, Market St, Guildford, Surrey GU1 4 LB
Miles Hellon, 27 Clerkenwell Close, London EC1R OAT
Douglas Hollick, 3 Antrim Terrace, Totnes, S. Devon TQ9 5QA
Martin Huggett, The Old Maltings, Stour St, Manningtree, Essex CO11 1BE
Lewis Jones, 109 Grove Hill, London E18 2HY
Nicholas Keen, Lamel Towers, 81 Hull Rd, York YO1 3JS
Mackinnon & Waitzman, 11 Sprowston Rd, London E7 9AD
Minns & Smart, Unit 5, 7 Westway, Oxford OX2 OJD
William Mitchell, Fircroft House, 760 Christchurch Rd, Bournemouth, Dorset BH7 6DB
Mark Ransom, 130 Westbourne Terrace Mews, London W2 6QG
John Rawson, 27 Clerkenwell Close, London EC1R OAT
Malcolm Rose, 1 The Mount, Rotherfield Lane, Mayfield, Sussex TN20 6AS
John Storrs, Hunston, Chichester, W. Sussex PO20 6NR
Whelpdale, Maxwell & Codd, 47 Conduit St, London W1R ODS
Andrew Wooderson, 119 Flaxton Rd, London SE18 2EW

SUGGESTED LISTENING
Bach: Brandenburg Concerto No. 5
Bach: Harpsichord Concertos
Scarlatti: Harpsichord Sonatas
Handel: *The Messiah* (Recitatives)
Fitzwilliam Virginal Book
Martinu: Harpsichord Concerto
Falla: Harpsichord Concerto
Henze: *Lucy Escott Variations* (for solo harpsichord)

SUGGESTED STUDY
Boxall: *Harpsichord Method* (Schott)
Nurmi: *Plain and Easy Introduction to the Harpsichord* (University of New Mexico Press)
Scott: *Playing the Harpsichord* (Harvard University Press)

POSTSCRIPT
'At the Great Room in Spring-Garden, near St. James's Park, Tuesday, June 5, will be performed a grand Concert of Vocal and Instrumental

Music. For the Benefit of Miss Mozart of Eleven, and Master Mozart of Seven Years of Age, Prodigies of Nature; taking the Opportunity of presenting to the Public the greatest Prodigy that Europe has to boast of. Every Body will be astonished to hear a Child of such tender Age playing the Harpsichord in such Perfection – and it is hard to express which is more astonishing, his Execution upon the Harpsichord, playing at Sight, or his own Composition.'

The Daily Advertiser, 31 May 1764

The Organ is the king of the instruments.
WOLFGANG AMADEUS MOZART

Organ

Popularity Rating: 13/16

The Pipe Organ can look back upon two thousand glorious years of existence.

Unlike the Piano, it produces its sound by forcing air through pipes, either manually (rare these days) or electrically. There are two or more keyboards, called manuals. Your feet play on another keyboard, called the pedalboard. Hand-operated stops (switches) enable the player to choose from a wide spectrum of tone colours. You can, for instance, obtain fair representations of the Trumpet, the Flute, the Oboe, the Clarinet and, almost, the human voice.

The natural progression from Piano to Organ is obvious. If you can play a Bach Prelude and Fugue satisfactorily, if the tone of the Organ thrills you, if you think you will enjoy the constant attention to the mechanics, then the Organ is for you.

Amongst the members of your team – family, friends, teachers, yourself – there should be one or more who can give you an introduction to a church organist. He might be prepared to let you have access to the Organ, at regular intervals, and might be willing to teach you. In fact, you and your team will find it comparatively easy to trace the right kind of teacher. You can shop around by visiting several churches and listen. Have a chat with the organist. Is he friendly? Will he let you watch him

15

at work? Has he taught pupils who are now organists themselves? Is he forthcoming with advice? Will he teach you? Can you afford the fee? If all the answers are positive, say yes.

Go into this with your eyes open. Operating a Pipe Organ is at first as complicated as driving a super-charged McLaren round a race track. And when you think you have mastered the intricacies of one particular Organ, you will meet fresh challenges in playing another, for no two instruments are exactly alike. Furthermore, you will probably have to put up with near arctic conditions for several months each year. Few churches will be heated all through autumn and winter.

You are still undeterred? Then here is the good news. Much preliminary practice can be done on your Piano at home. You may even have a pedalboard fitted to your instrument, so that you can do a great deal of the initial work at your leisure, before refining it at the Organ console.

The *Chamber Organ* is a miniature Church Organ, suitable for installing in the home. So is the *Electronic Organ*, which takes little space. In the absence of pipes, the sound of the Electronic Organ is produced by means of a circuit which allows for the signals emanating from the keys to be amplified and delivered through a loudspeaker or set of speakers. *

Proficient organists can hope for engagements, at first in smaller churches (on smaller instruments), in pop groups and even in funeral parlours.

Here is a list, not exhaustive of course, of Organ manufacturers:

Bontempi, Fraser St, Burnley, Lancs BB10 1UL
Bower, The Homestead, Three Hammer Common, Neatishead, Norwich NR12 8BP
Casio Electronics, Unit 6, 1000 North Circular Rd, London NW2 7JD
Classic Organs, Boxhill Rd, Boxhill, Tadworth, Surrey KT20 7SF
Elka-Orla, 3–5 Fourth Ave, Bluebridge Industrial Estate, Halstead, Essex CO9 2SY
Hammond Organs, 42 Blundells Rd, Bradville, Milton Keynes, MK13 7HF
Harrison & Harrison, Hawthorn Terrace, Durham DH1 4EJ
Hill, Norman & Beard, 134 Crouch Hill, London N8 9DX
Hohner, 39–45 Coldharbour Lane, London SE5 9NR
Irish Organ Co, Steeple Rd, Industrial Estate, Antrim, Co Antrim, N. Ireland

* Examinations in playing the Electronic Organ are offered by Trinity College of Music (Initial to Grade 5), Guildhall School of Music and Drama (Preliminary to Grade 8) and by the London College of Music (Introductory to Grade 8).

Johnson Organs, Gosforth Rd, Osmaston Industrial Estate, Derby, DE2 8HU

Kimball Europe, 38 Wigmore St, London W1H 9DF

Lowrey International, 26–28 Broomhills Industrial Estate, Braintree CM7 7PU

Makin Organs, Compton House, Franklin St, Oldham OL1 2DP

Mander Organs, St Peter's Organ Works, St Peter's Close, Warner Place, London E2 7AF

Norwich Organs, 395 Sprowston Rd, Norwich NR3 4HY

Peter Collins Organs, South Common, Redbourn, Herts AL3 7NB

Roland UK, Gt West Trading Estate, 983 Gt West Rd, Brentford, Middx TW8 9DN

Rose Morris, 32–34 Gordon House Rd, London NW5 1NE

Rushworth & Dreaper, 72 St Anne St, Liverpool L3 3DY

Starmer Shaw, 31 Whiteland Rd, Northampton

Walker & Sons, Wimbledon Ave, Brandon, Suffolk IP27 0NF

Willis & Sons, 87–91 Rushes Rd, Petersfield, Hants GU32 3AT

SUGGESTED LISTENING
Organ works by Bach, Buxtehude and Franck
Handel: Organ Concertos
Haydn: Organ Concerto
Mendelssohn: Organ Sonatas
Schumann: Organ Fugues
Saint-Saëns: Third Symphony
Elgar: Organ Sonata in G major
Holst: *The Planets*
Mahler: Second Symphony
Hindemith: Organ Sonatas
Messiaen: *Messe de la Pentecôte*

SUGGESTED STUDY
Alcock: *The Organ* (Primer) (Novello)
Baker: *The Complete Keyboard Player* (electronic) (Music Sales)
Baker: *The Complete Organ Player* (electronic) (Music Sales)
Davis: *The Organist's Manual* (Norton)
Dupré: *Method for the Organ* (Leduc)
Keeler/Blackham: *Basic Organ Techniques* (Kalmus)
Keller: *The Art of Organ Playing* (Peters) (in German)
Lang: *Exercises for Organists* (Novello)
Richter/Ware: *Adult Organ Course* (Kalmus)
Routh: *Playing the Organ* (English Universities Press)

POSTSCRIPT
There let the pealing organ blow,
To the full-voiced quire below,
    In Service high, and anthems clear
As may, with sweetness, through mine eare,
Dissolve me into ecstasies,
And bring all Heaven before mine eyes.

John Milton, *Il Penseroso*

Harp

Popularity Rating: 16/16

The Harpist, like the cat, walks alone. Except when Wagner demands a group of harps, or when another modern composer is satisfied with two, the exponent of this ancient instrument makes a lonely, if picturesque figure.

THOMAS RUSSELL, *Philharmonic*

The Harp is adored by music lovers everywhere, and its small band of dedicated players worship it. Yet it comes last in our popularity ratings. Small wonder, for the obstacles would dishearten all but the most determined.

- Expect to pay at least £6000 for a modern Concert Harp.
- The cost of a set of strings is appr. £200.
- You need a large estate car or van to transport a Harp.
- It takes two strong people to load and unload it.
- There are not many teachers, though you are likely to find only competent ones.
- The Harp repertoire is not very extensive.
- Strong fingers are essential, for a 7-lb pull is needed to play a medium loud note. Anticipate blisters.
- The Harp and its case take up considerable space, being at least 5 ft tall and 4 ft wide.

If you are still undismayed, look at the plus points.

- As a harpist, you have the pick of quite a number of orchestras you may wish to grace with your presence.
- The thrilling sound of the instrument is seductive. No harpist ever parts with it.
- Harpists are in great demand, not only as orchestral players but as accompanists to singers. If you have a pleasant voice, you will love accompanying yourself.
- Welsh and Irish Festivals offer opportunities for making music with fellow harpists.
- Non-pedal Harps, such as the Clarsach, are far less expensive than the Concert Harp and are accepted by Associated Board and Trinity for their Grade 1 to 3 examinations.

The modern Harp was perfected by Sébastien Érard in 1810. It has 46 or 47 strings and is tuned in the key of C flat major. The C strings are red, the F strings black or blue, to help you find your way. With its range of 6½ octaves, the Harp has the widest compass of all orchestral instruments. The tuning process is laborious and requires skill and patience. Not for the concert harpist the conviviality before a concert and the cool glass of lager in the interval, for the instrument needs tuning at both times.

The Harp rests against the player's right shoulder, though the weight is taken by the knees. This position brings the shorter strings (high notes) close to the player's right hand, and the longer strings (low notes) close to the left hand. The little fingers are not used at all. As the fingers pluck the strings, the strings vibrate and the soundboard amplifies the vibrations.

There are seven pedals, one for each diatonic note of the scale. The left foot operates B, C and D, and the right foot E, F, G and A. Depressing a pedal by one notch causes its strings to sound a semitone higher. Depressing it by a further notch raises the sound by a whole tone. Therefore:

Pedal	*Resultant note*
C pedal in high position	C flat
C pedal one notch down	C
C pedal two notches down	C sharp

Harp music is written, like Piano music, on two staves. In fact, pianists often make successful transitions from their instrument to the Harp.

Where financial considerations rule out the Concert Harp, the student may well start on a non-pedal instrument, such as the Clarsach,

Troubadour, Grecian or Gothic Harp. These smaller and cheaper instruments have fewer strings and are easier to learn. Their range is about four octaves, and the pitch of each string can be raised a semitone by a simple hand-operated mechanism.

These are some approximate current prices:

Concert Harps

Salvi Orchestra	£6500	
Salvi Symphony	£7700	
Salvi Aurora	£8200	
Salvi Diana	£9000	
Morley Etude	£6900	
Morley Orpheus	£7420	
Morley Delphi	£9650	
Wilfred Smith	£6000	Hire: £100 per month

Non-pedal Harps

Salvi Renaissance	£800	Hire: £65 for 3 months
Salvi McFall	£1210	Hire: £100 for 3 months
Morley Hempson	£720	
Morley Celtic	£1050	
Wilfred Smith Clarsach	from £475	Hire: £18 per month
Wilfred Smith Troubadour	from £630	Hire: £25 per month
Wilfred Smith Grecian	from £2200	Hire: £35 per month
Wilfred Smith Gothic	from £3000	Hire: £45 per month
Pilgrim Clarsach	£950	

Useful addresses include:

Salvi Harps: Holywell Music Ltd, 151–157 City Rd, London EC1V 1JH (Tel. 01 253 3738)

Morley: Morley Galleries, 4 Belmont Hill, London SE13 5BD (Tel. 01 852 6151)

Wilfred Smith: 15 Castelnau, London SW13 9PR (Tel. 01 748 6991)

Pilgrim Harps: Stansted House, Tilburstow Hill Rd, South Godstone, Surrey RH19 8NA (Tel. 0342 893242)

SUGGESTED LISTENING

Mozart: Flute and Harp Concerto

Liszt: *Mephisto Waltz* No. 1

Tchaikovsky: Waltz of the Flowers, from *Nutcracker Suite*

Sibelius: *Swan of Tuonela*

Debussy: *Danse sacrée et danse profane*

Saint-Saëns: *Fantaisie* op. 95
Fauré: *Impromptu* op. 86
Ravel: *Introduction et allegro*
Glière: Harp Concerto
Hindemith: Harp Sonata
Britten: *Ceremony of Carols*
Britten: Folk Songs with Harp accompaniment

SUGGESTED STUDY
Grossi: *Harp Method* (Novello)
Renié: *Complete Method for Harp* (Leduc)
Rensch: *The Harp* (Duckworth)
Salzedo: *Modern Study of the Harp* (Novello)
Van Campen: *Tutor for the Celtic Harp* (Kalmus)
Watkins: *Complete Method for the Harp* (Boosey & Hawkes)

A useful information centre is the United Kingdom Harpists Association. Contact:

Angela Moore, 39 Villiers Close, Surbiton, Surrey KT5 8DN (Tel. 01 390 2634)

POSTSCRIPT
For God the father Almighty plays upon the HARP of
    stupendous magnitude and melody.
For at that time malignity ceases and the devils
    themselves are at peace.
For this time is perceptible to man by a remarkable
    stillness and serenity of soul.
Hallelujah from the heart of God, and from the hand of
    the artist inimitable,
And from the echo of the heavenly HARP in sweetness
    magnifical and mighty.

Christopher Smart, 'A Song to David'

Violin

*If we were all determined
to play the first violin,
we should never have a complete orchestra. Therefore
respect every musician in
his proper place.*

ROBERT SCHUMANN

'What made you take up the Violin?' Sarah C., aged fourteen, writes in reply, 'I had always wanted to play from when I was very little.'

Catherine C., aged twelve, is more specific. 'I had been to a concert when I was about seven, with a solo violinist in it, and I decided that I wanted one day to be as good as him. So I kept asking my mum to let me learn, and she let me.'

Hugh L., aged 11^{11}/$_{12}$ as he puts it, sounds a note of realism. 'I chose the Voilin because the noise of a string instarment is more bearaball.'

In all three cases it was the sound of the instrument which impressed the young listeners. It seems reasonable, therefore, for parents to expose their children to a variety of musical experiences at an early age. Repeated listening to, say, the solo Violin, the Cello, the Flute, the Bassoon, the French Horn, the Trumpet, the singing voice, the Keyboards, the Harp or Percussion can often lead to a powerful relationship between the child and its favoured instrument, as well as to a rejection of antipathetic sources of sound.

Unlike the instruments discussed under previous headings, the Violin comes in several sizes: full, three-quarter, half, quarter and eighth. There is even a tiny sixteenth size Violin which can be handled by very small infants, often taught in the context of the Suzuki method which will be discussed in a later chapter and of which this author is an enthusiastic advocate.

The Violin is held between chin and shoulder, and not supported by the left hand, as some folk imagine. The sound is produced by the bow being drawn across the strings. The resulting vibrations are transferred to the hollow body of the instrument which acts as an amplifier. The tone can be varied a great deal, according to the speed of bowing, the weight applied and the point where bow meets string. The correct pitch is obtained by the left hand *stopping* the strings, i.e. in effect shortening them, at certain strategic points. Remember, the shorter the string, the higher the pitch. Instead of bowing the strings, the player can also pluck them (pizzicato).

A quality bow, ideally made of pernambuco wood, is essential, otherwise the resulting poor tone will discourage the beginner. Fibreglass models have been quite successful. They do not warp, they are relatively cheap, and the normally arduous job of re-hairing is fairly simple. Other accessories needed are a strong case with a secure carrying handle, a music stand, a chin rest and a shoulder pad or rest (to assist in supporting the instrument), rosin which, applied to the bow, promotes the necessary friction between bow hair and strings, a mute, which is a device that diminishes the volume and alters the character of the sound, and a duster, to clean and polish the instrument before putting it back into its case.

The violinist needs a good ear to guide the fingers of the left hand to their exact position where they stop the strings; a fraction above or below that point produces faulty intonation. There are many ways of playing *out of tune*, but only one way of playing *in tune*. The section on Aural Training (chapter 3) offers practical help.

Another quality needed by the prospective violinist and his family is patience. Progress is inevitably slow, and much encouragement is required to ease the learner through the early months. The support team should realize the mechanical complexity of a correct bowing or plucking action (right hand), while simultaneously achieving the correct pitch (left hand). The Violin offers no handicap to left-handers, both hands being fully occupied. Results will not be quick, but audible progress can be made from lesson to lesson, from practice to practice, and the rewards are worth striving for. Violinists will never be short of suitable music to play, since the literature for the instrument is very extensive. Even at an early stage they will be made welcome in school ensembles, where the shortage of string players contrasts with the abundance of, say, clarinettists and flautists. By giving the young violinist easy parts to play, the school's music director will introduce him to the joys of corporate music making, an experience which few instrumentalists will ever forget. With growing skill and confidence new doors will open which may admit the string player to the dazzling peaks of the solo concerto and to that most intimate world of chamber music. With perseverance, talent and skilful tuition, he will rejoice in Elgar's Violin Concerto, in Beethoven's *Kreutzer* Sonata, in Haydn's String Quartets and in Bartók's *Divertimento for Strings*.

It is not essential for a beginner to receive individual tuition. Excellent results have been achieved by expert teachers who have developed successful group tuition methods (see chapter 2).

Take advice before purchasing an instrument. Resist the temptation to buy a second-hand Violin which is labelled *Stradivari*, especially if the name is typed. An instrument suitable for a beginner – that is, a reliable, well made one – will cost not much under £100. If you hire, expect to pay approximately £6 per month.

Here is a list of some (by no means all) manufacturers and suppliers of string instruments and accessories:

British Music Strings, Bedwas House Industrial Estate, Newport, Gwent NP1 8XQ (Tel. 0222 883904)

Guivier, 99 Mortimer St, London W1N 7TA (Tel. 01 580 2560)

Hidersine, 240a Wickham Rd, Croydon CRO 8BJ (Tel. 01 654 5525)

Hill & Sons, Havenfields, Great Missenden, Bucks HP16 9LS (Tel. 02406 3655)

How Industries, Unit 1, Morewood Close, Sevenoaks, Kent TN13 2HU (Tel. 0732 450838)

Lodge, Fiddlers Folly, Baughurst Rd, Ramsdell, Hants (Tel. 0256 850140)

Mackenzie, Pembroke Wharf, All Saints St, London N1 9RL (Tel. 01 833 1854)

Nashville Music Strings, 203 Ystrad Rd, Pentre, Rhondda, Mid Glam CF41 7PE (Tel. 0443 437928)

Prentice, The Mill, Ash Priors, Taunton, Som TA4 3NQ (Tel. 0823 432734)

Shepherd, 241 Wood Lane, London W12 (Tel. 01 743 8717)

Strings & Things, Unit 2, Chapel Rd, Portslade, Brighton BN4 1PF (Tel. 0273 420704)

Thibouville-Lamy, 60 Clerkenwell Rd, London EC1M 5PY (Tel. 01 253 6346)

Vincent Bach, Unit 23, Garrick Industrial Centre, Garrick Rd, London NW9 6AQ (Tel. 01 202 3711)

Voigt & Son, 71 High St, Lindfield, Sussex (Tel. 04447 3206)

Voigt, Paul, 14 Westbury Rd, Northwood, Middx (Tel. 09274 23995)

Wilson (Bows), 4 Sparhawk St, Bury St Edmunds, Suffolk IP33 1RY (Tel. 0284 67070)

Withers, 22 Wardour St, London W1V 3HH (Tel. 01 437 2894)

Prices
£50 will buy an elementary outfit which includes a tolerable bow and an unimpressive case, all made in China, though string adjuster and bridge are West German, and the case locks are Japanese. Its brand name is *Stentor Student*, and it comes in all sizes from full to sixteenth. Obtain particulars and current prices from:

Stentor Music, Blackborough Rd, Reigate, Surrey RH2 7EZ (Tel. 0737 240226)

This outfit can also be hired for £11 per quarter from:

Barratts of Manchester, 652 Chester Rd, Manchester M16 0RX (Tel. 061 872 0713)

Stentor Music also offer two more commendable outfits. *Stentor Student Graduate*, also Chinese, costs about £90, but comes in full, three quarter and half sizes only. The other is the *Stentor Conservatoire*, full size only at about £100. Both outfits are made in China. Another interesting outfit, labelled *Andreas Zeller*, comes from Romania and retails at about £90. All sizes except sixteenth are available. Superior instruments, costing from £150 to £350 without bow or case, and usually full size only, are also available from Stentor Music. These are made in West Germany, by such reputable makers as Franz Sandner and Adolf Andreas Sandner. Fibre-glass bows cost between £30 and £40, wooden ones between £12 (beware!) and £40, in the so-called student range. Brazilwood bows are in the region of £75, but for pernambuco add another £50.

If you are thinking of purchasing instrument, bow and case separately, the Japanese case (Stentor Music) at £40 is sturdy and seems reliable. Vincent Bach (see previous list) retails bows from £15 to £30, and cases between £40 and £50.

Japanese Violin outfits from three-quarter to sixteenth size can be hired for £16 per term from:

Chas. E. Foote, 17 Golden Square, London W1R 3AG (Tel. 01 437 1811)

Once you have obtained your instrument, be good to it. After a playing session, remember three tasks:

(a) Loosen the bow hair; if you forget, the bow may warp.
(b) Remove stray rosin with a duster.
(c) Wrap the instrument in some soft material, such as a scarf, to guard against scratches. Then put your Violin into its case and make sure the locks are engaged. Create a permanent home for it, away from radiators, out of the sunlight and, most important, nowhere near the orbit of little and big feet.

Sooner or later you will have to learn to tune your Violin. It is depressing for the beginner and his family to endure the whining of an ill-tuned instrument. If you are too young to learn the skill, it might be a good idea for an older member of the family to take a special tuning lesson from your teacher.

SUGGESTED LISTENING
Vivaldi: Violin Concertos, especially *The Seasons*
Purcell: *Golden Sonata*
Bach: Double Concerto
Mozart: Violin Concertos
Beethoven: Violin Concerto
Beethoven: *Spring Sonata*
Paganini: *24 Caprices*
Mendelssohn: Violin Concerto
Brahms: Violin Concerto
Elgar: Violin Concerto
Debussy: Violin Sonata
Sibelius: Violin Concerto
Berg: Violin Concerto
Tippett: Concerto for Double String Orchestra

SUGGESTED STUDY
Applebaum: *String Builder* (Belwin Mills)
Cohen: *Violin Method* (Novello) (the publishers also issue 3 cassettes and an instruction booklet to supplement the Violin Method)
Flesch: *Memoirs* (Rockliff)
Gere: *The Art of Playing the Violin* (Stainer & Bell)
Havas: *New Approach to Violin Playing* (Bosworth)
Herfurth: *A Tune A Day for Violin* (Chappell)
Joachim, ed. Jacobsen: *Violin School* (Schauer)
Mackay: *A Modern Violin Method* (OUP)
Rickard & Cox: *Sing, Clap and Play* Violin (OUP)
Sevcik: *Selected Violin Studies* (Breitkopf/Fentone)
Six Lessons with Yehudi Menuhin (Faber)

POSTSCRIPT
'I have wept only three times in my life: the first time when my earliest opera failed, the second time when, with a boating party, a truffled turkey fell into the water, and the third time when I first heard Paganini play.'

Rossini

The Viola is a philosopher, sad, helpful; always ready to come to the aid of others, but reluctant to call attention to himself. ALBERT LAVIGNAC

Viola

Popularity Rating: 11/16

At around 27½ in. in overall length, the Viola is a little larger than the Violin. Both instruments share the same technique of fingering and bowing. The Viola bow is heavier but of about the same length as the Violin bow. Whereas the violinist reads from the treble clef, the violist uses the alto clef. Most Viola players are converted violinists, the transition being fairly painless. Since the left-hand fingers must cope with extra stretches, due to the longer fingerboard, a strong little finger is desirable, as is a reasonably wide handspan.

The characteristic sound of the Viola is variously described as *melancholy, plaintive* and *possessing the warmth of the human voice*; its low notes as *sonorous, husky,* even *cavernous*; its high notes as *passionate*, and at times *nasal* and *strident*.

When the author asked several young Viola players what decided them to take up that instrument, he received the following replies:

'My mum' (Richard C., aged eleven).

'Because it's different' (Sarah G., aged eleven).

'I thought, why not? I'll have a go' (Carly L., aged twelve).

Three valid answers. *To be different* means, in this case, to find a quicker way into an orchestra. Although there is a shortage of Violin players in school orchestras, violists are even rarer, and since their music is usually easier to play, players of that instrument can look forward to an early admission to an orchestra and to chamber ensembles. *To be different* might also mean that the player is interested in twentieth-century music. Composers such as Mahler, Strauss, Shostakovich, Hindemith and Britten have all written enthralling music for the Viola, while the instrument itself has gained immensely in popularity and prestige, thanks to the pioneering work of such performers as Lionel Tertis, Bernard Shore and William Primrose.

Before deciding whether to switch from the Violin to the Viola, or even whether to start with the Viola (as adults often do), you should consider the pros and cons.

The solo literature for the Viola is minute compared with that for the Violin, although it is growing. Hence, opportunities for the soloist are bound to be infrequent. Some players also dislike coping with the unfamiliar alto clef, while those with really small hands and short arms

27

might find themselves at a disadvantage. On the other hand, the Viola player can always switch to the Violin, according to circumstances and as the mood dictates. The Viola is to the string section what the middle voices (alto and tenor) are to the choir, and that is where the wise choir director puts the most musical voices. They have to create a perfect blend with their colleagues higher up and lower down, without losing their identity. The same applies to the Viola player. Richard Wagner, who wrote exquisite inner parts for the Viola, was right when he told his orchestra, *'Ich habe die Bratschisten zu Menschen gemacht.'* ('I have turned you violists into proper human beings.')

As for purchasing or hiring a Viola, please consult the previous section on the Violin, where you will also find hints on the care and upkeep of the instrument.

SUGGESTED LISTENING
Mozart: *Sinfonia Concertante*, for Violin, Viola and Orchestra
String Quartets by Haydn, Beethoven and Brahms
Brahms: *Geistliches Wiegenlied*, for Alto and Viola
Berlioz: *Harold in Italy*
Elgar: *Enigma Variations*, Nos 6 and 12
Strauss: *Don Quixote*
Hindemith: Viola Sonata op. 11/4
Hindemith: Viola Concerto
Kodaly: *Hary Janos* Suite, 3rd movement
Bartók: Viola Concerto
Copland: Viola Concerto
Walton: Viola Concerto
Britten: Passacaglia, from *Peter Grimes*
Britten: *Young Person's Guide to the Orchestra*

SUGGESTED STUDY
Arnold: *The Young Violist* (Bosworth)
Carse: *Viola School* (Stainer & Bell)
Mackay: *A Modern Viola Method* (OUP)
Milne: *Playing the Viola* (Novello)
Nelson: *Right from the Start: Viola* (Boosey & Hawkes)
Vashaw & Smith: *Work and Play String Method: Viola* (Kalmus)

POSTSCRIPT
When I play on my fiddle in Dooney,
Folk dance like a wave of the sea;
My cousin is priest in Kilvarnet,
My brother in Mocharabuiee.

I passed my brother and cousin:
They read in their books of prayer;
I read in my books of songs
I bought at the Sligo fair.

When we come at the end of time
To Peter sitting in State,
He will smile on the three old spirits,
But call me first through the gate;

For the good are always the merry,
Save by an evil chance,
And the merry love the fiddle,
And the merry love to dance:

And when the folk there spy me,
They will all come up to me,
With 'Here is the fiddler of Dooney!'
And dance like a wave of the sea.

W. B. Yeats, 'The Fiddler of Dooney'

*'I want the thing that
makes that noise.'*
JACQUELINE DU PRÉ
as a toddler, when first
hearing a Cello

Violoncello

Popularity Rating: 6/16

Best known by its shorter name, the Cello made its first appearance in the sixteenth century. The celebrated instruments made by Amati of Cremona date from that period. A hundred years later the Cello found regular employment in small ensembles, where it provided the bass line. From the nineteenth century onwards composers revelled in exploiting the warm carrying power of the instrument. They wrote solo works for the cellist and gave him interesting parts to play in orchestral and chamber works.

The length of the Cello is approximately 4 ft. Its four strings, C – G – D – A, sound an octave below those of the Viola, and its compass is about four octaves. The fingering differs from that of the Violin and the Viola. On the Viola the interval between neighbouring notes being fingered is a whole tone, but on the Cello it is a semitone. Also, the thumb which is not employed in fingering the Violin and Viola can be used for that purpose on the Cello. Cello strings are made of metal or gut. The former are easier to tune, the latter have a more mellow sound. As with the other string instruments, the bow must be rosined to provide a grip on the strings. You can experiment by drawing a completely unrosined bow across the strings; you will be startled by the absence of any musical sound.

A retractable spike supports the Cello, though house-proud parents may object to the rather insignificant marks this thorny offshoot leaves behind. In that case, and also on slippery floors, an anchoring gadget is used in which the spike can rest securely and inoffensively. For tuning and care of the instrument please consult the appropriate observations in the Violin section.

The tone of the Cello is rich, warm, sonorous and noble throughout its range. Its resonance is enhanced when standing on the podium of a concert hall which itself acts as a soundbox. The same applies to the Double Bass. The available sizes are full, three-quarter, half, quarter, eighth and tenth.

Consider the following possible drawbacks before deciding whether the Cello is for you:

(a) As for all string instruments, a good ear is needed, in order to play in tune. A recent students' guidebook compares the Cello with the Violin and states, absurdly, that 'the same degree of accuracy is not required to play the instrument in tune'. Do not believe it.

(b) The Cello costs about three times as much as a Violin.

(c) Strong fingers are required for pressing the strings against the fingerboard.

(d) Small hands and vulnerable backs are decidedly unhelpful.

(e) The Cellist needs to cope with three clefs – bass, tenor and treble.

(f) The size and weight of the Cello present several hazards. It is liable to get knocked about, since it is harder to miss than the Violin or the Viola. It receives only scant protection from its soft carrying bag, while a hard case, desirable as it is, can be pricy; it also pushes the total weight above 20 lbs.

Now consider the advantages of learning to play the Cello:

(a) The literature for the instrument is vast and glorious.
(b) The playing position for the Cello is less demanding than that for the Violin.
(c) The instrument is easier to learn than the Violin, and the initial efforts are less painful.
(d) Admission to playing ensembles is quicker for the Cellist than for the Violinist.
(e) The instrument suits left-handers as well as right-handers.
(f) The Cello makes an ideal second instrument for keyboard players who are already familiar with two of its three clefs, enabling them to enjoy ensemble playing.

A Chinese Cello outfit, the *Stentor Student* (instrument, bow and soft bag), costs between £200 and £245 (Stentor Music: address in Violin section). Charles Foote (see Violin section) have two outfits on hire, a Czech instrument for £51 per term (4 months) and a Romanian one for £64 per term (4 months).

Bows start at £20 for the wooden, and at £30 for the fibreglass variety. Soft bags start at £11 for most sizes. Stronger ones range between £25 and £75. But for a fibreglass case (recommended) you will not get much change out of £200.

SUGGESTED LISTENING
Bach: *Six Solo Suites*
Haydn: Cello Concerto
Saint-Saëns: Cello Concerto in D major
Saint-Saëns: *The Swan*
Schumann: Cello Concerto
Dvořák: Cello Concerto
Brahms: Double Concerto for Violin and Cello
Brahms: Piano Concerto No. 2, second movement
Tchaikovsky: *Variations on a Rococo Theme*
Elgar: Cello Concerto
Shostakovich: Cello Sonata
Britten: Cello Symphony

SUGGESTED STUDY
Benoy & Burrowes: *Cello Method* (Novello)
Cole & Shuttleworth: *Playing the Cello* (Novello)
Eisenberg: *Cello Playing of Today* (Novello)

Piatti: *Cello Method* (Stainer & Bell)
Starker: *An Organized Method of String Playing* (Kalmus)
Tortelier: *How I Play, How I Teach* (Chester)

POSTSCRIPT
'Little John Barbirolli's habit of
borrowing a family Violin and wandering
all over the flat while scraping it,
exasperated his grandfather Antonio
who took a cab to a fiddle shop and
came back with a half-size Cello. "Play
that instead," he told the boy. "You
have to sit down to the Cello."'

The Observer, 6 July 1947

Double Bass

Popularity Rating: 15/16

*To complete the string family
there are the Double Basses,
who are the centre of a
constant struggle between dignity
and the grotesque.*

THOMAS RUSSELL

The Double Bass was first sighted in the sixteenth century. Since then it has undergone several transformations. The number of its strings has varied from just three to six, but has now settled down to four (although the five-string Bass is still around). In its earlier days the Double Bass was employed to reinforce the Cellos, by playing their melodic lines, or *doubling* them, an octave lower down. Hence the name.

Whereas the Violin, Viola and Cello have their strings tuned in fifths, the Double Bass strings, E – A – D – G, are tuned in fourths. Because of the length of its fingerboard the interval of a whole tone requires a stretch from first (index) to fourth (little) finger. The music for the instrument is written an octave higher than it sounds, in order to avoid a proliferation of leger lines. The Double Bass, therefore, is a *transposing* instrument (the notes as seen differ from the sound as heard: the player has to convert or *transpose* written pitch to actual pitch).

Four sizes are available: full, three-quarters, half and quarter. The latter, affectionately known as *Mini Basses*, are diminutive but their generous width permits an attractive, resonant sound. The short finger-board enables small fingers to produce their notes effectively and in tune. This instrument can be started by an eight-year-old. The other three sizes need a tall player. Since the Double Bass is likely to exceed its player in length, a comfortable handling position can be achieved by perching on a high stool. For transport purposes, a well padded, waterproof carrying case is a necessity.

The Double Bass, except when handled by jazz virtuosos, is not too strong on flexibility. Although professionals can manage some amazing runs, the instrument prefers a dignified, unruffled existence. Occasionally, however, the Double Bass steals the limelight. In the Scherzo of his Fifth Symphony, for instance, Beethoven requires the Basses to gallop at a fair lick, while Saint-Saëns, in his *Carnival of the Animals*, turns the player into a tipsy elephant.

Is the Double Bass your choice? Consider first the counter-indications. The instrument is bulky and, placed in its case, it needs a good deal of breathing space. It is a splendid friend when played, but a stubborn opponent when carried. It does not take kindly to public transport. Many students, however, solve this problem by using their teacher's instrument for their lessons, and their school or youth orchestra's basses for re-hearsals. A serious drawback is the scarcity of solo music; but if you will not mind this, you can relish the thought of contributing a solid foundation for the rest of the orchestra. The often prohibitive cost of a Double Bass must be taken into consideration, as well as its vulnerability (it is easier to hit than to miss). On the other hand, most beginners find it astonishingly easy to learn, since its music does not move rapidly and does not often require great agility.

If the Double Bass player will seldom perform solos, his playing opportunities are not restricted to the orchestral world, since both pop groups and jazz bands are interested in him. There is another bonus which many players relish. Since their hollow bellies (the instruments', not the players') act as sound boxes, the players will not only *hear* the music but *feel* its vibrations right inside their bodies.

Here are some representative approximate prices:

Firm	Instrument		Cost
Foote	Czech Outfit	½ size, ¾ size	£490
		Hire: 4 months	£80
	E. German Outfit	¾ size	£800
		Hire: 4 months	£130

Vincent Bach	3211	¼, ½, ¾ sizes	£550
	Cover		£45
	Bow		£55
Boosey & Hawkes*	400	½ & ¾ sizes	£410
	400 Outfit	½ & ¾ sizes	£465

SUGGESTED LISTENING
Beethoven: Fifth Symphony, Scherzo
Saint-Saëns: *Carnival of the Animals*
Schubert: 'Trout' Quintet
Rimsky-Korsakov: *Sheherazade*
Mahler: Symphony No. 4
Strauss: *Also sprach Zarathustra*
Varèse: *Octandre*
Ravel: *L'Enfant et les Sortilèges*

Jazz double bass: Jimmy Blanton, Ray Brown, Charlie Mingus, Oscar Pettiford

SUGGESTED STUDY
Bottesini: *Method for the Double Bass* (Yorke Edition)
Eugene Cruft School of Double Bass Playing (Joad Press)
Evans: *Basic Bass* (Novello)
Hertl: *Elementary School of Double Bass Playing* (Artia)
ed. Slatford: *Yorke Solos for Double Bass* (Yorke Edition)
   Yorkassette (demonstration recordings of above) (Yorke Edition)
Slatford & Pettitt: *The Bottom Line* (book for teachers) (Calouste Gulbenkian Foundation)
Vashaw & Smith: *Work and Play Bass Method* (Kalmus)
Ward: *Elementary Method for Double Bass* (Rubank)

POSTSCRIPT
'So powerful was the tone which Domenico Dragonetti could produce from his instrument, that I have frequently heard him pull the whole orchestra back with one accent if they wavered in the least.'

Henry Phillips, *Musical and Personal Recollections*

* Boosey & Hawkes: Deansbrook Rd, Edgware, Middx HA8 9BB (Tel. 01 952 7711).

34

*The Guitar speaks directly
to the heart with quiet
simplicity.*

ANDRÉS SEGOVIA

Guitar

Popularity Rating: 9/16

This section discusses the Classical Guitar, since the four major examining bodies restrict their graded examinations to that type. In a subsequent chapter details will be given of examination requirements for keyboard, orchestral and band instruments, but this is the appropriate place for surveying the syllabuses for the Guitar.

Board	Grades	Requirements
AB	1 to 8	3 Prepared Pieces – Scales and Arpeggios – Playing at Sight – Aural Tests. Grades 6 to 8: Theory of Music or Practical Musicianship Grade 5 must have been passed.
G	Prelim. to 8	3 Prepared Pieces – Scales and Arpeggios – Playing at Sight – Aural Tests – General Musicianship: oral questions on prepared pieces and general musical knowledge. Grade 8: Two-hour paper on Rudiments of Music (for exemptions consult syllabus).
T	1 to 8	3 Prepared Pieces – Scales and Arpeggios – Playing at Sight – Aural Tests – Viva Voce: oral questions on prepared pieces and (Grade 8) on their composers. Grade 8: written paper (for details consult syllabus).
L	Introductory to 8	3 Prepared Pieces – Scales and Arpeggios – Playing at Sight – Aural Tests – Viva Voce: oral questions on prepared pieces and, for higher grades, also on general musical knowledge. Grades 6 to 8: LCM Theory Grade 6 must have been passed (for exemptions consult syllabus).

At first glance, there does not seem to be much difference between the requirements of the various examination bodies. All prescribe Prepared Pieces, Scales and Arpeggios, Playing at Sight and Aural Tests. However, if we examine just one aspect, the Scales and Arpeggios, we find significant differences in the standard required for identical grades. Here is an example:

Scales and Arpeggios: Grade 4

	AB	G	T	L
major scales & range in octaves	F♯ G A♭ 2 B F 2 E 3	E G C 2 C in tenths 1	B F♯ D♭ G♭ 2	–
melodic minor scales & range in octaves	e c♯ d e♭ 2	d 2	g♯ b♭ e♭ 2	g 2
harmonic minor scales & range in octaves	e c♯ d e♭ 2 candidate's choice of melodic or harmonic	d 2	g♯ d♯ b♭ 2	–
chromatic scales & range in octaves	A B♭ C 2	–	A B♭ B C 2	D E♭ 2
slurred scales	–	–	A F 1	–
dominant sevenths & range in oct.	C D 2	–	D A 2	C 2
major arpeggios & range in oct.	B♭ C 2 E 3	A 2	E♭ A♭ D♭ 2	G 2

	AB		G		T		L	
minor arpeggios & range in oct.	f c d	2	e a	3 2	f# eb bb	2	c	2
cadences	–		E major		–		–	

It will be seen that Trinity College of Music sets its sights higher than the others, while London College of Music requires a great deal less. This may tempt you or your teacher to *shop around* when choosing your syllabus. This is not wise. Lighter requirements may well be compensated by heavier marking and vice versa. Consult the next chapter, which scrutinizes these and other aspects of graded examinations.

Your aim in sitting for a Guitar examination is not just to pass a particular grade, but to obtain an expert's assessment of your present standard. So, before sending off for your examination entrance form, ask yourself these questions:

1 Can you tune your own instrument accurately and reasonably quickly?
2 Has your tone a pleasant quality? Is it clear? Has it got sufficient volume?
3 Are your posture and your hand positions conducive to optimum effectiveness?
4 Do you use your hands for supporting the Guitar (which you should not!), or are they free for playing?
5 Is your left hand technique sufficiently assured to produce legato phrasing?
6 Do your strings buzz from time to time?
7 Is your playing *musical*, as opposed to *mechanical*?

All examiners, regardless of which board they represent, will be searching for the answers, so you had better find them first.

Life with your Guitar is fairly solitary, intimate and immensely rewarding. Reading its music is less demanding than reading Piano notation. Practising seldom presents a problem, since its devotees need little coaxing, while even the closest neighbours will hardly hear it. The cost of new and second-hand instruments can be quite moderate. Persons with various kinds of handicap may find fulfilment in studying the Guitar. This also applies to those whose unsure sense of pitch would debar them from most other instruments. BUT, contrary to popular theory, the Guitar is not easy. A well qualified teacher is as indispensable as is regular practice. As your skill develops, so will your desire to become a guitarist worthy of the name, one who can make magic when he plays a Bach Suite, a Fantasia by Dowland, an Andante by Sor, a Villa-Lobos Etude, a Scarlatti Sonata, a Valse by Ponce or one of the Estudios by Tarrega.

When looking for a second-hand Guitar, take an expert's advice, who will make sure that it is nylon-strung, that the strings are not far from the fingerboard (one eighth of an inch or less), and many other details unbeknown to the layman. Investing in a Guitar *case* rather than a soft *bag* is excellent policy, considering the instrument's vulnerability. Find out whether its lid opens widely and remains widely open, for Guitars are sometimes assaulted by their own protectors when they are taken out of or put back into their cases. Secure a place in your home for your loved one which avoids drastic changes of temperature and humidity. Keep it in its case before and after playing, away from radiators, fires and sunlight. Resist the temptation to hang it on the wall. It looks terrific, especially with a few embroidered ribbons dangling from its neck, but the author nearly lost a treasured instrument when it made an un-programmed descent. Some professionals combat dry atmospheric conditions by locking half a potato in the accessories compartment of their Guitar cases. It is worth a try. Also, examine your second-hand Guitar's fingerboard. If it is smutty, it will respond to cautious polishing, after the strings have been removed, with a few drops of linseed oil on 000 wire wool. The first re-stringing should be undertaken together with your teacher who will also show you how to tune your instrument.

Examples of current prices of new instruments:

Firm	Instrument	Cost	Rental
Foote	B & M Infanto, three-quarters outfit	£45	£9 (4 months)
	B & M Espana, full size outfit	£70	£14 (4 months)
Stiles	B & M Almeria	£50	
	Juan de la Mancha Allegro	£70	
Encore	ENC 40 N	£35	
	RCG 50 N	£40	
Stentor	Antonio Lorca	£100	
	Case	£45	

Addresses:
Chas. E. Foote, 17 Golden Square, London W1R 3AG
Stiles Music Centre, 272 Lewisham High Street, London SE13 6JX
Encore, John Hornby Skewes, Salem House, Garforth, Leeds LS25 1PX
Stentor Music, Blackborough Road, Reigate, Surrey RH2 7EZ

SUGGESTED LISTENING
Dowland: Lute Lessons (transcribed for Guitar)
Bach: Lute Suites (transcribed for Guitar)
Giuliani: Guitar Concerto
Ponce: Guitar Concerto
Turina: Guitar Sonata
Rawsthorne: *Elegy*
Berkeley: Guitar Concerto
Arnold: Guitar Concerto
Walton: *Five Bagatelles*
Britten: *Nocturnal*
Henze: *Kammermusik*
any music played by Segovia, Bream, Williams or Ghiglia

*Jazz guitar: Charlie Christian, Eddie Lang, Wes Montgomery, Django
Reinhardt, John Schofield*

SUGGESTED STUDY
A Tune A Day: *Classical Guitar* (Chappell)
Dardess: *Playing the Guitar* (Kalmus)
Duarte: *A Guitarist's ABC of Music* (Novello)
Duarte: *Foundation Studies in Classical Guitar Technique* (Novello)
Duarte: *The Young Person's Way to the Guitar* (Novello)
Gray: *Guitar from the Beginning* (Arnold)
Kennedy: *Junior Guitar* (Cramer)
Pairman: *Easy Stretch Guitar* (Stainer & Bell)
Quine: *Introduction to the Guitar* (OUP)
Ranier: *Guitar Method* (United Music)
Stimpson: *The Guitar* (OUP)
Bellow: *Illustrated History of the Guitar* (Ricordi)
(Video) *The Complete Guitar Player* (Stainer & Bell)

POSTSCRIPT
'A portable companion always ready to go where you go, a small friend
weighing less than a fresh born infant, to be shared with few or many, just
two of you in sweet meditation.'
                                                  Carl Sandburg, *The Guitar*

Flute

Popularity Rating: 3/16

The Flute is endowed with a character peculiarly its own and with a special aptitude for expressing certain feelings, in which it is matched by no other instrument.

HECTOR BERLIOZ, *Treatise on Instrumentation*

What can one say against the Flute? You have taken care, so far, to balance the advantages of learning to play a particular instrument against its disadvantages. The Flute offers a wealth of the former and an almost total lack of the latter. Its repertoire is vast, and you can even enlarge on it by playing a good deal of music written for the Violin, except the five lowest notes. Anyone who has ever played the Recorder – that is most of us – finds the transition to the Flute gratifying, since they have already mastered the basic fingering. Flute players read one clef only, the treble clef, and only one note at a time, whereas string players are often required to produce two, three or four notes simultaneously. No great physical strength is needed, while the development of a sound breathing technique – the essence of good tone production – benefits the player's health. More rapid progress can be expected on the Flute than on the Oboe or the Bassoon, all members of the same woodwind family. The initial outlay for purchasing or hiring is relatively small, and its upkeep straightforward. Tuning is simpler than on string instruments. To flatten the pitch, you pull the mouthpiece away from the body of the instrument; to sharpen it, you push them closer together. There are no transport problems, and you can practise the Flute anywhere without fear of disturbing the neighbours.

Are there no snags at all? Pronounced left-handers could find themselves at a disadvantage. Some dizziness can accompany the initial blowing efforts. Also, promotion to an orchestra may take time, due to the popularity of the instrument. End of snags.

The best time for starting to learn the Flute is not determined by your age but by the length of your arms. Run a measuring tape along a stick, starting at its end, and mark it at 26", the length of a Flute. Hold the marked section as you would hold a Recorder, left hand above right. Now swing the stick over to the right of your face, and put your lips to an imaginary hole in the stick. Hold it horizontally, with your hands still in the fingering position. If your left arm is long enough to reach easily across your body, without allowing the stick to dip towards the floor, and if you can achieve this with your neck comfortable and straight, then you are ready for the Flute.

40

Although the Flute is a member of the *woodwind* family, it is now generally made of metal. A wooden body produces a more mellow tone, but a metal one secures greater carrying power with enhanced brightness.

You coax the Flute into sound by blowing *across*, not *into*, an oval hole. This sets the air inside the hollow body vibrating. The length of that column of air determines the pitch, and you can regulate the length by covering or uncovering the holes which are set along the body of the Flute. You achieve this by manipulating felt-padded, spring-loaded keys which open and close those holes.

The tone of the Flute is limpid and clear, bright and penetrating in its higher register, and often uncannily like a faraway Trumpet on its ten lowest notes. It revels in rapid passages, and flautists are indebted to Theobald Boehm who, in 1847, created the modern instrument with its intricate set of keys mounted on rods. A hundred years before Boehm many Flutes sported only one or two keys.

You maintain your instrument in good order by wiping its interior as soon as you have finished playing, and by periodic lubrication of its key mechanism and joints.

A special bonus awaits you once you have conquered the Flute, for you will also be able to play its smaller version, the Piccolo. Both instruments share the same system of fingering, but the Piccolo sounds one octave higher. Its notes are written an octave lower, to avoid too many leger lines. The sound is brilliant, but rather shrill at the top. Listen to the final movement of Beethoven's Fifth Symphony for the uplift and exhilaration this little fellow can generate.

Before considering purchasing or hiring a Flute, obtain as much information as you can by contacting manufacturers and distributors. Here is a list (Woodwind and Brass) which does not claim to be comprehensive:

All Flutes Plus, 5 Dorset St, London W1H 3FE
Barratts of Manchester, 652 Chester Rd, M16 ORX
Boosey & Hawkes, Deansbrook Rd, Edgware, Middx HA8 9BB
Cooper, 15 Grandison Rd, London SW11 6LS
Fletcher Coppock & Newman, Morley Rd, Tonbridge, Kent
Flutemakers Guild, 10 Shacklewell Rd, London N16 7TA
Howarth, 31 Chiltern St, London W1M 1HG
James, 5a Dorset St, London W1M 3PE
Bill Lewington, 144 Shaftesbury Ave, London WC2H 8HN
Myatt, 55 Nightingale Rd, Hitchin, Herts SG5 1RE
Paxman, 116 Long Acre, London WC2E 9PA
Pro/Brass, 2 Highgate Rd, London NW5 1NR

Rose Morris, 32 Gordon House Rd, London NW5 1NE
Rudall Carte, Deansbrook Rd, Edgware, Middx HA8 9BB
Stentor Music, Blackborough Rd, Reigate, Surrey RH2 7EZ
Tradewind, PO Box 377, Braintree, Essex CM7 4EA
Vincent Bach, Unit 23, Garrick Ind. Centre, Garrick Rd, London NW9
  6AQ
Ward & Winterbourn, 75 Alexandra Rd, London NW4 2RX
Woodwind, 208 Liverpool Rd, Cadishead, Manchester M30 5DB
Woodwind & Brass, 55 Nightingale Rd, Hitchin, Herts

A popular instrument, and rightly so, is the *Yamaha* Flute. Prices for
the 221N and 221S models are £325 and £356 respectively. You can hire
them for four months from Bill Lewington (for this and other addresses
see List) for £54 and £59 respectively. The same firm offers a cheap
Hsinghai Piccolo for £103, and a better quality one, the *Yamaha 32*, at
£317 (rental terms £17 and £53 respectively for a period of four months).
An inexpensive American Flute is available at £150 from Pro/Brass,
while Paxman's models start at £200. The *Buffet* Flute is on offer for £305
from Woodwind & Brass, and Stentor Music sell the *Armstrong* Flute in
the price range £295 to £400. All-Flutes-Plus retail a wide variety of
models, starting at £230. Their rental charges range from £32 per term
for a £230 model to £52 for one retailing at £358. Reasonable carrying
cases start at £20. As for second-hand instruments, expect to pay around
65 per cent of the cost of a new one.

Proficient flautists may wish to join the British Flute Society, which
promotes recitals, master classes and lectures. In the past, such distinguished performers as James Galway, William Bennett and Jean Pierre
Rampal have lectured and played to members of the society. Contact:

Membership Secretary, 65 Marlborough Place, London NW8 OPT.

SUGGESTED LISTENING
Bach: *Six Sonatas* for Flute
Gluck: Dance of the Blessed Spirits, from *Orfeo*
Mozart: Concerto for Flute and Harp
Beethoven: Symphony No. 6
Rossini: *William Tell* Overture
Debussy: *Prélude à l'Après-midi d'un Faune*
Debussy: *Syrinx*
Stravinsky: *Octet* for Wind Instruments

Piccolo
Tchaikovsky: Chinese Dance, from *Nutcracker Suite*
Dubensky: *Capriccio for Piccolo*
Kodály: *Harry Janos* Suite

SUGGESTED STUDY
A Tune A Day for Flute (Chappell)
Gariboldi: *Complete Method* (Leduc)
Hugues: *Flute School* (Ricordi)
Klosé: *Complete Method* (United Music)
Learn As You Play Flute (Boosey & Hawkes)
Lyons: *Take up the Flute* (Chester)
Oboussier: *Workbook for Woodwind Groups* (Novello)
Pugliese: *Elementary Method for Flute* (Ricordi)
Waddington: *The Well-Tempered Flautist* (Piper Publications)
Wye: *A Beginner's Practice Book for the Flute* (Novello)

Books
Chapman: *Flute Technique* (OUP)
Boehm: *The Flute and Flute Playing* (Dover)

Video
Discovering the Flute (Cramer-Utopia)

POSTSCRIPT
'But that which did please me beyond anything in the whole world was the wind-musique when the angel comes down, which is so sweet that it ravished me, and indeed, in a word, did wrap up my soul, so that it made me really sick, just as I have formerly been when in love with my wife; that neither then, nor all the evening, going home, and at home, I was able to think of anything, but remained all night transported, so as I could not believe that ever any musick hath that real command over the soul of man as this did upon me: and it makes me resolve to practise wind-musique, and to make my wife do the like.'
Samuel Pepys, *Diary*

Oboe

The Oboe is an ill wind that nobody blows good.

GROUCHO MARX

Popularity Rating: 8/16

The hauntingly beautiful notes of the Oboe come at a price. Can you afford over £500 for a new instrument, or £80 for a three months' hire period? If so, read on and give thought to further obstacles. You need fairly thin lips. If yours are thick, you had better consider another instrument. It will take quite some time before you can produce an acceptable sound. If you are impatient for quick results, turn elsewhere. Also, do not consider the Oboe if you have respiratory problems or suffer from high blood pressure. You need good ears. Since the Oboe is seldom completely in tune with itself, perfect pitch can only be achieved by lip control and breathing.

Now reflect on the benefits. The tone of the Oboe is ravishing, and the accomplished player regards his instrument as a loyal friend for life. All orchestras will welcome the oboist and make much of him. The repertoire for this instrument contains some exquisite music and is fairly extensive.

The characteristic tone of the Oboe is often described as rich, luscious, expressive, pungent, bitter-sweet, dulcet and slightly nasal. In its higher register it is a little thin but has great penetrating power. When played slowly, it assumes a melancholy quality. You can hear the Oboe at the beginning of an orchestral concert when it sounds its 'A' for the rest of the orchestra to tune to.

The Oboe is a double-reed instrument. The reed is formed from two thin pieces of cane, approximately 3″ long, which are bound together and fitted to a staple (a little metal tube). The whole fits into the top of the instrument. To create a sound you force your breath through the narrow slit between the reeds. This makes them vibrate against each other, and causes the column of air inside the hollow body of the instrument to vibrate and thus to produce a note. Before he starts playing the oboist sucks his reed to moisten it, in order to achieve a responsive note. Hence the saying, 'whet your whistle'. The range of the Oboe is about two and a half octaves, half an octave less than that of the Flute.

Most Oboes are fashioned from rose, grenadilla or cocus wood, but cheaper models are made of manufactured material, such as ebonite. When taken apart, the three sections of the Oboe fit into a fairly small carrying case. Daily upkeep includes cleaning each section with a special feather until dry, and wiping the keys with a soft duster.

The present Oboe has a venerable past. Its forerunner was the ancient Greek double-reed pipe, the *Aulos*. In the Middle Ages this had developed into the *Shawm* (Latin: *calamus* = reed), which can be regarded as the ancestor of the modern Oboe. The name derives from the French *Hautbois*, which means 'loud wood'. In the nineteenth century the instrument received the intricate key mechanism which distinguishes it today.

Closely related to the Oboe is the Cor Anglais or English Horn, which is neither English nor a Horn. The fingering is the same as for the Oboe, and the skilled oboist can easily switch from one instrument to the other. The tone of the Cor Anglais is plaintive and nostalgic. It sounds a perfect fifth lower than the Oboe and is a transposing instrument. Its notes are written a fifth above their actual sounds. In other words, when the oboist reads the note C, he also plays that note; but when the Cor Anglais player reads C, he plays the F below. Since the Cor Anglais is six inches longer than the Oboe, its metal tube which holds the double-reed is bent back towards the player, to promote a comfortable playing position.

Consult the following table, which quotes current prices of both instruments and its accessories. The firms have been picked at random, and you are advised to obtain further quotations from the much fuller list which appears in the Flute section.

Firm	Instrument	Cost	Rental
	OBOE		
Lewington	Hsinghai 1119	£505	£85 (4 months)
	Orsi 89S	£630	£105 (4 months)
	Conservatoire	£1380	
Ward & Winterbourn	Student Model S	from £520	
Howarth	Howarth	£475	£75 (3 months)
	Howarth B	£525	£80 (3 months)
	Bundy	£500	£75 (3 months)
	others	£655 to over £4000	
Vincent Bach	1472	£630	£95 (3 months)
	1293	£630	£95 (3 months)
	Reeds		
Lewington	£3.80		
Howarth	£4.25 upwards		

	Case
Ward &	£35 (wood)
Winterbourn	£49 (resin)
Howarth	£30 upwards
Vincent Bach	£42

	COR ANGLAIS	
Lewington	Conservatoire	£2110
Howarth	Howarth S20	£1325
	Howarth S20C	£1355

	Case
Ward &	
Winterbourn	£45
Howarth	£43

SUGGESTED LISTENING
Albinoni: Oboe Concerto
Bellini: Oboe Concerto
Mozart: Oboe Quartet
Grieg: Morning, from *Peer Gynt*
Elgar: Symphony No. 2, slow movement
Strauss: Oboe Concerto
Delius: *La Calinda*
Britten: *Six Metamorphoses after Ovid*

Cor Anglais
Wagner: *Tristan und Isolde*, Prelude Act Three
Dvořák: Symphony *From the New World*, slow movement
Sibelius: *Swan of Tuonela*
Copland: *Quiet City*
Alwyn: *Autumn Legend*

SUGGESTED STUDY
A Tune A Day: *Oboe* (Chappell)
Barrett: *Complete Method* (Leduc)
Brod: *Complete Method* (Lemoine)
Oboussier: *Workbook for Woodwind Groups* (Novello)
Rothwell: *The Oboist's Companion* (OUP)
Sellner: *Oboe Method* (Kalmus)
Skornicka: *Instrumental Course: Oboe* (Boosey & Hawkes)
Voxman: *Rubank Elementary Method* (Rubank)

Books
Bartolozzi: *New Sounds for Woodwind* (with record) (OUP)
Rothwell: *Oboe Reed Making* (Nova Music, formerly OUP)
Goossens/Roxburgh: *Oboe* (Macdonald & Janes)

POSTSCRIPT
Sir Thomas Beecham on a visit to a country churchyard read an inscription, 'Here lies a great musician and a superb oboist.' He shook his head and muttered, 'How on earth did they manage to get both of them into this small grave?'

There is no other wind instrument which can produce a tone, let it swell, decrease and die away as beautifully as the clarinet.
HECTOR BERLIOZ,
Treatise on Instrumentation

Clarinet

Popularity Rating: 4/16

Johann Denner, citizen of Nuremberg, got tired of making Flutes for the rich (noblemen) and the poor (musicians). He envisaged a woodwind instrument which could well do without the sweet tone of the Flute, but would have greater carrying power combined with the bright ring of the Trumpet. So Denner redesigned the popular *Chalumeau*, a reed pipe, and gave it a *speaker key*, which is an extra hole which extended the upper range of the instrument. Since the clear tone of his new instrument reminded him of the Trumpet (or *Clarino* in Italian), he called it *Little Clarino* or *Clarinet*. All that was 300 years ago.

The first major composer to love and cherish the Clarinet was Mozart. Listen to his Clarinet Concerto and see whether you can resist its spell.

In the middle of the last century, a key mechanism was added, and the modern Clarinet was born.

In contrast to the Oboe, the Clarinet has a *single* reed. This is gripped by the *ligature*, a circular metal clamp with screws, and fitted over a hole in the mouthpiece, causing vibrations inside the body of the instrument and thus producing the sound. There are four sections to the Clarinet: the mouthpiece and barrel, the upper joint, the lower joint and the bell.

Like the Piccolo and the Cor Anglais, the Clarinet is a *transposing instrument*. It is pitched in B flat and it sounds a tone below the written note; that is to say it will play an F when it sees the note G. There is also a Clarinet in A which sounds a tone and a half (three semitones) below the written music; that is to say it will play an E when it sees the note G. The existence of both instruments enables composers to make the clarinet-tist's life easier by avoiding too many sharps and flats. Generally, the Clarinet in A is used for sharp keys, and the Clarinet in B flat for flat keys.

Players and listeners describe the tone of the Clarinet as bright, brilliant, liquid and clear. Its high notes can be piercing, even strident, while the low notes – the *chalumeau* register – have a rich, oily, and somewhat sinister quality. The Clarinet is extremely agile and rejoices in rapid runs and wide leaps all over its extensive range of almost four octaves.

Adjustments to the pitch are made by slightly pulling the tuning barrel *out* to flatten the pitch, or *in* to sharpen it. When you have finished playing, the reed should be removed from the mouthpiece, and both must be wiped dry. Then reverse the process and put the cap on.

The two great attractions of this instrument are its comparatively low purchase price and its user-friendliness. The beginner can achieve rapid progress, provided he is not deterred by occasional appalling squawks which occur when he least expects them. The popularity of the Clarinet may make it difficult to gain early admission to an orchestra, but there are social playing opportunities elsewhere. Clarinettists are needed in Wind Orchestras, in Woodwind Ensembles, in Clarinet Choirs, and in Wood-wind Quartets, apart from those exhilarating playing sessions with a piano accompanist. In addition, there is the wide world of jazz and pop at the clarinettist's fingertips.

When buying a new instrument, do not automatically choose the cheapest models. These are often made of insufficiently seasoned wood, and you can expect future trouble in the shape of cracks. Synthetic materials have proved quite successful, and your prospective teacher will advise on the best buy. Here are a few examples of current models and prices:

Firm	Instrument	Cost	Rental
Paxman	Buffet	£220 upwards	
Pro/Brass	Plastic	£135	
	Wood	£200	

Lewington	Yamaha	£277 to £1015	£46 (4 months)
	Noblet	£507 to £1884	£84 (4 months)
	Leblanc	£942 to £1240	
Stentor	Armstrong	£245	
Vincent Bach	Resonite	£229	£34 (3 months)
	Wood	£365	£55 (3 months)

SUGGESTED LISTENING
Mozart: Clarinet Concerto
Mozart: Clarinet Quintet
Weber: Clarinet Concerto
Weber: Overture to *Freischütz*
Mendelssohn: Overture to *Midsummer Night's Dream*
Brahms: Clarinet Quintet
Stravinsky: *Ebony Concerto*
Strauss: *Duet Concertino* for Clarinet and Bassoon
Gershwin: *Rhapsody in Blue*

Jazz clarinet: Sidney Bechet, Eddie Daniels, Johnny Dodds, Benny Goodman, Jimmy Giuffre

SUGGESTED STUDY
A Tune A Day: *Clarinet* (Chappell)
Brymer: *The Way to Play* (Chappell)
Harris: *Cambridge Clarinet Tutor* (CUP)
Harvey: *The Complete Clarinet Player* (Wise Publications)
Kell: *Kell Method for Clarinet* (Boosey & Hawkes)
Klosé: *Complete Method for Clarinet* (Leduc)
Learn As You Play Clarinet (Boosey & Hawkes)
Lyons: *Take up the Clarinet* (Chester)
Oboussier: *Workbook for Woodwind Groups* (Novello)
Staats: *New Imperial Method for Clarinet* (Kalmus)
Tschaikov: *Play the Clarinet* (Chappell)

Books
Bartolozzi: *New Sound for Woodwind* (with record) (OUP)
Thurston: *The Clarinet* (Cramer)
Thurston: *Clarinet Technique* (OUP)
Weston: *The Clarinettist's Companion* (Fentone)

Advanced students will find it worth their while to contact the Clarinet and Saxophone Society, 167 Ellerton Rd, Tolworth, Surrey KT6 7UB.

POSTSCRIPT
Once more he stept into the street
And to his lips again
Laid his long pipe of smooth straight cane;
And ere he blew three notes (such sweet
Soft notes as yet musicians' cunning
Never gave the enraptured air)
There was a rustling that seemed like a bustling
Of merry crowds justling at pitching and hustling,
Small feet were pattering, wooden shoes clattering,
Little hands clapping and little tongues chattering,
And, like fowls in a farmyard when barley is scattering,
Out came the children running.
All the little boys and girls,
With rosy cheeks and flaxen curls,
And sparkling eyes and teeth like pearls,
Tripping and skipping, ran merrily after
The wonderful music with shouting and laughter.

Robert Browning, *The Pied Piper of Hamelin*

Bassoon

Popularity Rating: 14/16

Toscanini had a legendary gift of memory. Once he had read a score he knew it by heart. A Bassoon player once told him, as the opera was about to begin, that his E flat key was broken, but that a new Bassoon was coming for the second act. 'There is no E flat in the Bassoon part in the first act,' Toscanini reassured him.
News Chronicle, February 1936

How would you like to play the *Bundle of Firewood?* or the *Fagotto* as the Italians call it? That is to say, the Bassoon. Bundle of Firewood, because it dismantles into five sections. If you are interested, you should be able to say yes to the following questions:

1 Can you afford £700-plus for a new instrument?
2 Have you got a good ear?
3 Are your hands large and are your fingertips broad?
4 When playing in an orchestra, would you enjoy providing the bass line for the others to revel in their melodies?

If you have answered no to the first question, take heart. Many schools, youth orchestras and music centres keep a Bassoon of their own. Locate one and impress its keeper with your enthusiasm. He may lend it to you, provided you find a teacher, practise conscientiously and, later, join his orchestra.

Although your hands must be generously proportioned in order to reach the keys and cover the holes, the blowing effort is far more comfortable than for the Oboe, and bassoonists are known to make rapid progress. The instrument looks big, but it fits into a case not much larger than a Violin case. Its weight is supported by a sling or a spike. Do not expect a big tone from the Bassoon. It is a gentle beast, honey-voiced, warm, mellow, slightly comical on staccato notes, reedy and cavernous in its lower range. Like the Oboe, it is a double-reed instrument.

Apart from the joy of playing with a piano accompanist, the Bassoon player will invariably be most welcome in orchestras and woodwind ensembles, while further playing opportunities exist in smaller chamber groups, such as a woodwind quartet (Flute, Oboe, Clarinet, Bassoon).

The eight-foot-long Bassoon tube is doubled back upon itself, thus reducing the length to a manageable four and a half feet. Bassoon music is written largely in the bass clef, but uses the tenor clef for the upper notes of its range of over three octaves.

When it had outgrown its unwieldy, long-legged ancestor, the *Bass Shawm*, the Bassoon acquired its first keys in the seventeenth century. By the time Mozart and Beethoven wrote for it, it had eight keys. Today it boasts a system of twenty-one.

As a bassoonist you ride two horses: solo passages and bass lines. The former provide the limelight, the latter the glory; for the Bassoon is often called upon to provide the fundament for the orchestral structure, and your good ear will enable you to blend well with your colleagues and to enhance their performance.

Here are a few samples of current prices:

BASSOON

Firm	Instrument	Cost	Rental
Howarth	Lafleur	£690	£103 (3 months)
	Lark (Chinese)	£575	£86 (3 months)
	Case	£85 upwards	
Lewington	King Tempo	£795	£135 (4 months)
	Monnig Sonora	£1685	
Vincent Bach	Resonite Outfit	£1420	£213 (3 months)

SUGGESTED LISTENING
Vivaldi: Bassoon Concertos (38 altogether)
Mozart: Bassoon Concerto
Weber: Bassoon Concerto
Elgar: *Romance* for Bassoon and Orchestra
Dukas: *The Sorcerer's Apprentice*
Hindemith: Bassoon Sonata
Poulenc: Trio for Oboe, Bassoon and Piano
Arnold: *Fantasy* for Solo Bassoon

SUGGESTED STUDY
Allard: *Bassoon Method* (Kalmus)
A Tune A Day: *Bassoon* (Chappell)
Bourdeau: *Grande méthode complète* (English) (Leduc)
Oubradous: *Complete Method for Bassoon* (Leduc)
Skornicka: *Instrumental Course: Bassoon* (Boosey & Hawkes)
Voxman: *Rubank Elementary Method for Bassoon* (Rubank)

Books
Spencer/Mueller: *The Art of Bassoon Playing* (Kalmus)
Waterhouse: *The Proud Bassoon* (EUP)

POSTSCRIPT
In 1745 a performance took place, at Lincoln's Inn Fields Theatre, London, of a sonata for twenty-four Bassoons and four Contra Bassoons.

Music is your own experience,
your thoughts, your wisdom.
If you don't live it, it won't
come out of your Sax.
CHARLIE PARKER

Saxophone

Popularity Rating: unavailable

Jacqueline G., aged fifteen, lives in Kent and plays the Tenor Saxophone with gusto and no little skill. When asked what decided her to take up that instrument, she replied, 'I saw a man in our local park dressed up as a pink panther, playing the *Pink Panther* on a Tenor Sax. That did it.' The interview continued:

Q: What do you remember about your first lesson?
A: I got introduced to my teacher's cat.
Q: Do you enjoy practising?
A: Yes. It's better than doing homework. And all the neighbours can hear me.
Q: To what group or orchestra do you belong?
A: My school orchestra, the local Junior and Senior Bands, the district Youth Orchestra, the National Children's Wind Orchestra and the County Youth Wind Orchestra. But I haven't made the National Youth Jazz Orchestra yet.
Q: What of the future?
A: I want to be a nuclear physicist and play the Sax in nightclubs.

Clearly, the Saxophone is for living, even though it ruined its inventor.
    Adolphe Sax, a Belgian maker of Clarinets, lived in Paris in the last century. His research into creating instruments with a more powerful tone than could be obtained from his Clarinets had led him to the invention of the Saxophone, in about 1840. Sax combined features of the Oboe, the Clarinet and the brass family, using the conical bore of the first, the single reed of the second, and the metal body of the third. The result was a lusty mongrel which recalled its forebears' distinctive characteristics. In fact, the litter he bred consisted of fourteen specimens of varying shapes. Military bands soon adopted the Saxophone, and Sax won several prizes, showing off his brood at the Great Exhibition at London's Crystal Palace in 1851. Alas, fortune deserted him. He went bankrupt and was forced to sell his whole stock, together with his workshops and showrooms. He did not live to see the Saxophone's triumphant entry into the world of jazz, in 1920, where performers such as Benny Carter, Charlie Parker, Coleman Hawkins and Lester Young

later developed their virtuoso technique, allied to the hallmark of Jazz and the Saxophone: *improvisation*.

Of the original fourteen instruments only six are in general use today, the Sopranino in E flat, the Soprano in B flat, the Alto in E flat, the Tenor in B flat, the Baritone in E flat and the Bass in B flat. Of these, the Alto and Tenor are the most popular by far. Since all share the same system of fingering, you can play all once you can play one. The range of each type is 2½ octaves, and *all* read from the treble clef.

The Saxophone is a transposing instrument. Music for the Alto is written a major sixth above the actual pitch. Therefore, when the player reads the note C, he plays E flat below. Music for the Tenor is written a major ninth above the actual pitch. Therefore, when the player reads the note C, he plays B flat an octave and a tone down.

The Saxophone is not difficult to learn. In fact, this is one instrument which many students can teach themselves, provided they take occasional consultation lessons. The tone production is easier than on the other reed instruments, and the fingering is similar to the Recorder and the Flute. Players of those instruments and of the Clarinet usually find a transition to the Saxophone quite straightforward. No undue finger stretches are involved, and the instrument can be played by people with small hands. Its weight is supported by a neck strap, but if you have back or shoulder problems, take medical advice first. If your lips are thin and/or if you have small front teeth, you start with a handicap, owing to the Saxophone's requirements for tone production. A good ear is essential, for the instrument is not perfectly in tune with itself and requires the player's constant vigilance.

A great stumbling block, unfortunately, is the cost (see examples of current prices further on). It is possible, however, to procure reasonably priced second-hand instruments, provided you keep away from the obsolete *high-pitch* variety. Do not worry over small dents, but check whether you can clearly read the engraved identification on the bell. If you cannot, it has been relacquered, and you will want to know why.

Cleaning is effected by passing a swab through the dismantled sections, while the normal adjustments extend to the occasional repair of pads. There is not much more to the upkeep and care.

Players and listeners describe the tone of the Tenor Saxophone as rich, throaty, oily, thick and powerful. The instrument preserves its characteristic tone in mixed ensembles, where it does not blend well with its colleagues. Nature (and Monsieur Sax) meant it to be its own master.

Ample playing opportunities exist for the Saxophonist. School orchestras often make a pet of him, since he can substitute for cellists, bassoonists, hornists and others who may be unavailable. He can join jazz and dance bands, pop groups, symphony orchestras, wind orchestras, military bands, and he can play chamber music in Saxophone trios and quartets (Alto – Tenor – Baritone, and Soprano – Alto – Tenor – Baritone respectively).

Examples of current prices:

Firm	Instrument	Cost	Hire
Myatt	Buffet S1 Tenor	£950	ask for
	Buffet S2 Alto	£995	current
	Buffet Prestige Tenor	£1425	terms
	second-hand, recent offers	from £220 up	
Paxman	Champion Alto	£450	ask for
	Yamaha S23 Alto	£475	current
	Jupiter Tenor	£565	terms
	Yamaha S23 Tenor	£790	
Boosey &	B & H 400 Alto	£500	
Hawkes	Buffet Evette Alto	£600	
	B & H 400 Tenor	£600	
	Buffet Evette Tenor	£700	

Advanced students will find it worth their while to contact the Clarinet & Saxophone Society (details in Clarinet section).

SUGGESTED LISTENING
Bizet: *L'Arlésienne*, Prelude
Glazunov: Saxophone Quartet
Strauss: *Sinfonia Domestica* (employs Sax quartet!)
Ravel: *Bolero*
Stravinsky: *Ebony Concerto*
Walton: *Façade*
Britten: *Sinfonia da Requiem* (*Dies Irae* section)
Gershwin: *An American in Paris*
Muldowney: Saxophone Concerto

Jazz saxophone: John Coltrane, Charlie Parker, Sonny Rollins, Lester Young

SUGGESTED STUDY
A Tune A Day: *Saxophone* (Chappell)
Bumcke: *Saxophone Method* (Schauer)
Geckeler: *Belwin Saxophone Method* (Belwin-Mills)

Klosé: *Méthode Complète: Saxophone* (English) (Leduc)
Langey: *The Saxophone* (Boosey & Hawkes)
Ravenscroft: *The Complete Saxophone Player* (Music Sales)

Improvisation
Marshall: *Take Up Jazz* (Chester)

Cassettes
Saxophone Examination Repertoire (through Lewington)

POSTSCRIPT
Music teacher to third form: 'Put the word *syncopation* into an explana-
tory sentence.' Tony's effort reads: 'My dad plays the Sax during the
week, but on Saturday nights he goes in for syncopation.' Bewildered
teacher asks Tony to clarify. 'Well, sir. My dictionary says, "syncopation
– *the unsteady progress from bar to bar.*"'

Recorder

*A good recorder
sets all in order.*
Old Proverb

Popularity Rating: unavailable

What do you think of the following statements?

1 The Recorder is very easy to learn.
2 Music for the Recorder dates back to Handel's time.
3 The Recorder is for younger children.
4 The Recorder is the cheapest of all instruments.
5 The Recorder is a solo instrument.
6 The Recorder is an instrument for the whole family.

The correct answer to all six questions is yes/no.
1. The Recorder is easy to learn initially, *but* only patience, a good ear
and dedication can turn you into an advanced player.
2. Handel, Bach, Alessandro Scarlatti, Vivaldi, Telemann and

Corelli all composed music for the Recorder, *but* so did Britten, Tippett, Arnold, Rubbra, Hindemith and Berio in our time.

3. Young children make friends with the Recorder in no time, *but* more and more older boys and girls, adults and handicapped people of all ages are discovering the joy of playing this instrument, on their own and with their fellow creatures.

4. True, you can buy a reasonable instrument for a few pounds, *but* a Steenbergen Descant Recorder, made of grenadilla wood, costs £359, while an Oberlander Bass Recorder in boxwood is priced at £516.

5. The Recorder's solo repertoire is inexhaustible, but a special thrill awaits you when you team up with other players, especially a Recorder Consort, i.e. Descant, Treble, Tenor and Bass.

6. In the sixteenth, seventeenth and eighteenth centuries the Recorder was regarded as a household instrument and, in the absence of television, families would make music together as a matter of course. Sadly, and to the detriment of family life, this is no longer so.

You may agree that a revival of that charming custom is overdue. *

As your playing becomes more fluent, you may wish to avail yourself of further playing and learning opportunities offered by *holiday courses*. Here are some addresses to contact:

Baroque Chamber Music Week, 4 Glebe Gdns, Grove, Wantage, Oxon OX12 7LX

Beamish Hall College, Stanley, Co. Durham DH9 ORG

Benslow Music Trust, Little Benslow Hills, Ibberson Way, Benslow Lane, Hitchin, Herts SG4 9RB

Dolmetsch Summer School, Marley Copse, Marley Common, Haslemere, Surrey GU27 3PU

Edinburgh Early Music Centre, Edinburgh Academy, Henderson Row, Edinburgh EH3 5BL

Morley College, 61 Westminster Bridge Rd, London SE1 7HT

North East Early Music Forum, 28 Wentworth Rd, York YO2 1DG

Northern Recorder Course, 41 Grosvenor Rd, Sale, Cheshire M33 1WL

Northumbrian Recorder and Viol School, 58 Mayfield Rd, Whitby, N. Yorks YO21 1LX

Old Rectory, Fittleworth, Pulborough, W. Sussex RH20 1HU

Recorder in Education Summer School, 2 Meadowhead Close, Sheffield S8 7TX

Theobalds Park College, Waltham Cross, Herts EN7 5HW

* Fact File III presents an easy teach-yourself method for the whole family.

West Dean College, West Dean, Chichester, PO18 OQZ
Westham Adult College, Barford, Warwickshire CV35 8DP

If there remains any lingering doubt about the 'respectability' of the
Recorder, remember that all major examining bodies have adopted it for
their graded examinations. The following Table provides details:

Board	Instrument	Grades	Requirements
AB	Descant	1 to 6	Aural Tests – Prepared Pieces –
	Treble	1 to 8	Scales and Arpeggios – Playing at Sight. For Grades 6 to 8: Theory of Music Grade 5 must have been passed.
G	Descant	Prelim. to 5	Aural Tests – Prepared Pieces – Scales and Arpeggios (not for
	Treble	1 to 8	Preliminary) – General Musicianship (oral questions on prepared pieces and, from Grade 4 onwards, on rudiments of music and allied topics) – Playing at Sight. Grade 8 requires a two-hour paper (exemptions for Ass. Bd Grade 5 Theory, or GCE Music, or GCSE Grade 1 level).
T	Descant	1 to 5	Aural Tests – Prepared Pieces –
	Treble	1 to 8	Scales and Arpeggios – Viva Voce (oral questions on prepared pieces, rudiments of music and allied topics) – Playing at Sight. Grade 8 requires a pass in TCM Theory of Music or TCM Musicianship Grades 5, 6, 7 or 8 (exemptions for GCE Music).
L	Descant	Prelim. to 6	Aural Tests – Prepared Pieces – Scales and Arpeggios – Viva
	Treble	Prelim. to 8	Voce (as above) – Playing at Sight.

Some current prices († = plastic):

Firm	Descant	Treble	Tenor	Bass
Aulos	£10†	£15†	£40†	£175†
Dolmetsch	£5†	£15†	£35†	£600
	£25	£40	£70	
Hellinger	£10	£30	£41	
Kung	£75	£150	£200	£405
Moeck	£25	£60	£105	£270
Mollenhauer	£30	£70	£125	£375
Rahma	£5†	£15†	£35†	
Schneider	£40	£70	£105	
Yamaha	£5†	£10†	£40†	£370
	£50	£60	£105	

SUGGESTED STUDY
Bergmann: *Descant Recorder Lessons* (Faber)
Bonsor: *Enjoy the Recorder* (Schott)
Bonsor: *Enjoy the Treble Recorder* (Schott)
Davey: *Recorder Playing In Colour* (Chappell)
Dolmetsch: *Advanced Recorder Technique* (Arnold)
Imogen Holst: *The Book of the Dolmetsch Recorder* (Boosey & Hawkes)
Pease: *Recorder For All* (Cramer)
Pitts: *Recorder From the Beginning* (Arnold)
Pitts: *Treble Recorder From the Beginning* (Arnold)
Priestley & Fowler: *School Recorder Book* (Arnold)
Salkeld: *Play the Recorder* (Chappell)
Winters: *Read and Play* (Stainer & Bell)
Young: *Method For Recorder* (Rubank)

SUGGESTED LISTENING
Vivaldi: Recorder Concerto in C major
Vivaldi: Concerto for Recorder and 2 Violins
Vivaldi: Recorder Sonatas
Telemann: Suite in A minor for Recorder and Strings
Handel: Recorder Sonatas, op. 1
Sammartini: Recorder Concerto
Hindemith: Recorder Trio
Rubbra: Recorder Sonatina
Berkeley: Recorder Sonatina
Berio: *Gesti*

Any music played by Carl Dolmetsch, Frans Brüggen, David Munrow, Hans-Martin Linde.

POSTSCRIPT
'To Drumbleby's and did there talk a great deal about pipes, and did buy a recorder which I do intend to learn to play on, the sound of it being of all sounds in the world most pleasing to me.'
Samuel Pepys, *Diary*

French Horn

Little Boy Blue,
Come blow your horn.
The sheep's in the meadow,
The cow's in the corn.

Popularity Rating: 12/16

Elephants, antelopes, gazelles, boars, stags and rhinos – such is the distinguished pedigree of this instrument. Over the centuries, holes were bored into its body, animal horn gave way to metal, mouthpiece, crooks and valves were constructed, and the modern French Horn, twelve feet of coiled tubing, had arrived. It now presents a greater challenge to its prospective player than did its ancestors to the hunter.

Be warned, everything seems to discourage you from learning to play this instrument.

1 It is very expensive (see below).
2 It is probably the hardest instrument to learn.
3 It will never become easy.
4 It requires an extremely good sense of pitch.
5 Imperfect teeth and/or thick lips are a distinct handicap.

There is a bright side, however, if you look hard enough. Although a new instrument costs at least £600, schools and youth orchestras will often provide one on loan (see section on Bassoon). Also, there is a fairly extensive second-hand market.

True, the French Horn is difficult to learn – your lips do most of the work – but it can be done, provided:

(a) you have good ears;
(b) you develop an efficient breathing technique;

(c) you are prepared to make daily practising your chief hobby;
(d) you are in love with its sound.

Yes, everything hinges on this last point. Listen to one of Mozart's Horn Concertos or to Britten's *Serenade for Tenor, Horn and Strings*, preferably played by Dennis Brain, Alan Civil or Barry Tuckwell. Their sound is warm, noble, melancholy, mellow, romantic and utterly bewitching. If its spell truly ensnares your imagination, then nothing may deter you from joining the select company of students of this aristocratic instrument.

The literature for the French Horn is inexhaustible, and the ability to play it carries with it a pass to any ensemble, such as symphony orchestras, wind orchestras, brass ensembles and chamber groups. Proficient players may wish to join the British Horn Society, which promotes festivals, lecture recitals and courses. Contact:

The Secretary, British Horn Society,
116 Long Acre, London WC2E 9PA (Tel. 01 240 3642)

The French Horn in F is a transposing instrument. Thus, when the player reads C, he sounds the F below. The bass clef is used for the lower notes, and the treble clef for the higher ones. A most useful instrument is the Double Horn. This possesses an extra valve which turns the instrument into a dual purpose one, in the keys of F and B flat, allowing a somewhat easier access to the high notes. The compass of the French Horn is a most respectable 3½ octaves, matching the range from the trombonist's bottom notes to approximately the trumpeter's top.

A special study of deep breathing and support from the diaphragm, as practised by professional singers, is as indispensable as impeccable aural control. The reader is referred to the sections on Singing (p. 82) and Aural Tests (p. 120) for further information.

Care of the instrument involves wiping the exterior and interior surfaces, and lubricating the valves and tuning slides. The mouthpiece is cleaned with a bristle brush. Most important – do not eat before playing! Otherwise your shining Horn will turn into a waste bin.

Examples of current prices:

Firm	Instrument	Cost
Myatt	Anborg	£600
	Yamaha YHR 313	£895
	second-hand	from £195

Firm	Instrument	Cost
Boosey & Hawkes	B & H 400	£840
Paxman	Paxman Studenti	£565
	Lidl	£655
	Cases: plywood	£60
	moulded	£95
	fibreglass	£140
Lewington	Yamaha YHR with case	£935
Vincent Bach	Sonora with case	£750

(Ask for details of hire charges.)

Having bought, rented or borrowed your instrument, do insure it. One of the companies specializing in this field is:

Brass Band Insurance Services, 312 High St, Harlington, Hayes, Middx UB3 5BT (Tel. 01 759 0825)

SUGGESTED LISTENING
Handel: *Water Music*
Mozart: Four Horn Concertos
Tchaikovsky: Symphony No. 5
Brahms: Horn Trio
Wagner: *Siegfried* (Siegfried's Horn Call in Act Two)
Strauss: Two Horn Concertos
Tippett: Sonata for Four Horns
Britten: *Serenade for Tenor, Horn and Strings*

SUGGESTED STUDY
A Tune A Day: *French Horn* (Chappell)
Huth: *Method for Horn* (Schauer)
Langey: *The French Horn* (Boosey & Hawkes)
Moore & Ettore: *A French Horn Primer* (Belwin Mills)
Rattner: *Elementary Method for the French Horn* (Chappell)
Skornicka: *Elementary Method for French Horn* (Rubank)
Tuckwell: *Playing the Horn* (OUP)

Farkas: *The Art of Horn Playing* (Kalmus)
Schuller: *Horn Technique* (OUP)

POSTSCRIPT

'At one rehearsal session at the BBC . . . we began rehearsing XYZ's Symphony for its first broadcast performance. The composer himself was in attendance . . . We hadn't been rehearsing very long when colleagues at either side were using strong adjectives to describe the horrible noise, for no melody or harmony for that matter had yet appeared. Suddenly our Principal (Horn) turned to me and said, "Bob, play it in C, Frank, play it in E natural, Peter, play it in E flat and I'll play it in D." We were approaching a unison passage, whereupon we all four horns lifted our bells and blew like mad. You never heard such a row. XYZ didn't seem to notice.'

as told by a former Horn player with the BBC Symphony Orchestra

---

For the Trumpet of God is a blessed intelligence,
And so are all the instruments in Heaven.
CHRISTOPHER SMART, *A Song to David*

Trumpet

Popularity Rating: 7/16

Well over 3300 years ago the Egyptian Pharaoh Tutankhamun was laid to rest in his pyramid tomb. As tradition would have it, two watchmen with the loudest voices in the land were interred with him. In 1923, some curious archaeologists decided mankind had waited long enough. They opened the burial chamber and they found not only the Pharaoh, but his two watchmen – a pair of richly ornamented Trumpets. Being very early instruments, they had no mouthpieces, but bulging protuberances, not unlike bottle tops. One was made of silver, the other of bronze and gold, and both had the Pharaoh's name engraved on them. The BBC had the instruments examined by an expert who succeeded in wakening those watchmen from their long slumber. They answered with blaring voices, one blowing a whole tone higher than the other. The BBC recorded their sound, and the contemporary *Radio Times* carried the amazing story of Tutankhamun's Trumpets, under the headline TUT'S TOOTS.

As the Trumpet developed over the centuries, the aura of majesty remained with it. Its clarion calls would sound at court, in battle and at public festivities. It would lead the ceremonies in church and at the opera, its fanfares announced the birth and death of princes. When the Trumpet was at last admitted to the orchestra, it lost its independence. No longer would it cause horses to rear and hearts to pound. It now was required to work as a member of a team, to sound in harmony with others. The eagle had been caged.

Two momentous innovations created the modern Trumpet. In the eighteenth century it was fitted out with *crooks*. These are extra lengths of tubing, easily attached to the instrument and enabling it to play in different keys. Players, however, found it a little cumbersome and time-consuming to change crooks every time they wanted to change key. So Friedrich Blühmel and Heinrich Stölzel of Berlin came to the rescue. In 1818 they patented their *Kastenventil*, a system of three valves, operated by the player's right hand. By pressing a single valve or any combination of three, extra lengths of tubing are called into operation and the player can change key in an instant.

You produce your tone by forcing a stream of air through the mouthpiece. This causes the air inside the instrument to vibrate, with the result that a sound emanates at the other end. Careful lip control – tensioning and slackening – is needed to achieve the desired pitch and timbre. The Trumpet is a transposing instrument, its key being B flat. Therefore, when you read the note C, you sound a B flat. There are also Trumpets in other keys, but they are seldom used, except for the Trumpet in C which is gaining in popularity. The latter is non-transposing, and you play what you read. The range is 2½ octaves, from the F sharp below middle C to the C above the treble stave, though experts can soar higher.

Care and upkeep include wiping the exterior surfaces, cleaning the mouthpiece and the tuning slides with a bristle brush, and swabbing the interior of the valve casing. Your teacher will demonstrate the mechanics of all this, as well as the soapy water treatment.

The Trumpet attracts a large following. It is as bright to look at as it sounds. It is easier to learn than string or woodwind instruments, with the possible exception of the Clarinet. It is less expensive than its colleagues, the French Horn, Trombone and Tuba. Since it appears in full orchestras, wind orchestras, brass bands, brass ensembles, brass quartets, dance and jazz bands, and in pop groups, playing opportunities are abundant. However, you need to be fit. High passages can be fatiguing, due to the demands on your lip muscles. Also, your teeth and gums should be healthy. If you are less than fully fit, try the less demanding Cornet (see p. 72). A sense of humour also helps, for playing in a hall produces a see-saw effect: as the temperature rises –

think of the audience gasping while they admire your performance – the metal expands and the pitch rises. The player has to watch out for this and take appropriate action. But during those lengthy rest periods which sympathetic composers provide for brass players, the metal cools again and the pitch drops. Again, counter-measures are required. Make your sense of pitch as perfect as possible (see section on Aural Tests), and you will enjoy being in control.

Examples of current prices:

Firm	Instrument	Cost
Boosey & Hawkes	B & H 435-1-0	£135
	B & H 435-2-0	£180
	B & H 437-1-0	£275
Paxman	Paxman Studenti	£200
	Bach Mercedes II	£300
	second-hand with case	from £150
Stentor	KG 600	£300
	KG 601	£330
Vincent Bach	Sonora 135L	£125
	Bundy 1530	£310
Lewington	Parrot	£93
	Yamaha YTR 2320 with case	£321
Pro/Brass	Caravelle 512	£169
	Musica	£135
Myatt	Champion	£112
	Besson 600	£359
	second-hand	from £75

(Ask for details of hire terms.)

SUGGESTED LISTENING
Bach: Brandenburg Concerto No. 2
Clarke: Trumpet Voluntary
Handel: 'The trumpet shall sound' (from Messiah)
Haydn: Trumpet Concerto
Hummel: Trumpet Concerto
Rossini: Overture William Tell
Verdi: Grand March from Aida
Wagner: Overture Rienzi
Shostakovich: Trumpet Concerto
Britten: Fanfare for St Edmundsbury (for 3 Trumpets)
Birtwistle: Concerto for Trumpet, Vibraphone and Strings

Jazz trumpet: Louis Armstrong, Miles Davis, Dizzy Gillespie, Wynton Marsalis

SUGGESTED STUDY
Arban: *Complete Trumpet Method* (Leduc)
A Tune A Day: *Trumpet* (Chappell)
Baines: *Brass Instruments* (Faber)
Dale: *Trumpet Technique* (OUP)
King: *The Brass Player's Guide* (Belwin Mills)
Langey: *The Trumpet* (Boosey & Hawkes)
Ridgeon: *Brass for Beginners* (Belwin Mills)
Rubank: *Elementary Method for Trumpet* (Rubank)
Skornicka: *Instrumental Course: Trumpet* (Boosey & Hawkes)
Snell: *The Way to Play: Trumpet* (Chappell)
Wastall: *Learn As You Play: Trumpet* (Boosey & Hawkes)

POSTSCRIPT
'Mr William Lang, soloist in the Haydn Trumpet Concerto, has culti-
vated a true Esterhazy style. This was a captivating performance, with
smooth, golden notes hanging in mid-air.'
Evening Standard

'William Lang's performance was marred by coarseness of tone and
untidy detail.'
Daily Telegraph

Trombone

Popularity Rating: 10/16

*If everyone is in a
frisky spirit, the spirit
gets to me and I can make
my trombone sing.*
JIM ROBINSON, *Hear Me Talkin' To Ya*

Haydn wrote a *Surprise* Symphony, but Beethoven knew how to surprise,
stun and electrify his audiences, all at the same time. Listen to the
opening of the last movement of his Fifth Symphony, as it blinds the
listener like blazing fire. The simplest melody in C major is proclaimed by
the full orchestra:

What is it then that so rouses audiences everywhere, almost two centuries after that music had first burst upon its listeners? Beethoven provides the answer. 'The last movement', he wrote, 'has three Trombones . . . it will make more noise than six Kettledrums, and a better noise at that.' The resourceful composer had not used the Trombones in his first, second and third movements. He saved their majestic entry for his majestic finale. Perhaps fear of showing our emotions prevents us, as we listen, from jumping up like King George I, when he heard the Hallelujah Chorus from Handel's *Messiah*. Such is the power of music, and of the Trombone in particular.

It can sound dignified, fierce, sombre, grandiose, serene or swaggering, at the composer's and the player's choice. The tone is produced by causing the column of air inside the instrument to vibrate, but instead of shortening and lengthening the tubing by means of valves, this is usually achieved by extending and retracting a movable slide. The player's ear and nothing else tells him how far to extend or to retract. If the slide is allowed to travel its whole length without interruption, the result is a remarkable glissando, so beloved by jazz musicians. The nimble *valved* Trombone, something of a rarity these days, was much admired by Verdi and is still used in some bands.

Curiously, the Trombone has experienced little change during its lifespan of almost seven centuries. It started its career under the name *Sackbut*, looking much the same as it does today. It normally appeared in groups of four or eight, and Monteverdi composed some delicious music for them. Since its tone reminded listeners of the Trumpet, it was soon called Trombone, Italian for *big trumpet*.

Two types of Trombone appear in symphony orchestras, the Tenor in B flat, and the Bass in G. Both require the same playing technique, so when you have mastered one, you can also play the other. The range of both types is just over 2½ octaves.

The Bass Trombone is a non-transposing instrument. So is the Tenor, when written in the bass clef. But when you play from the treble clef, your sound is a major ninth below the written note. In other words, reading C produces the B flat a ninth below.

Care of the instrument includes disassembling, wiping exterior and interior surfaces, and lubricating the playing and the tuning slide.

Although the solo repertoire is restricted, playing opportunities include full orchestra, brass ensembles of every kind, dance and jazz bands. The learning process presents no major problem, due to the Trombone's straightforward mechanics. But though your fingers have no actual work to do, your ears must be very alert. Do not consider the Trombone, until your sense of pitch is really reliable. Thin lips, so desirable in an oboist, are not much help here. If yours are fairly fleshy, you are off to a good start.

Examples of current prices:

Firm	Instrument	Cost	Hire
Vincent Bach	Sonora 3058L Outfit	£225	£34 (3 months)
	Bundy 1523 Outfit	£320	£48 (3 months)
Lewington	Parrot 6421	£105	£17 (4 months)
	Meister MSL 3058	£200	£33 (4 months)
Myatt	Corton	£140	ask for details
	Accord	£235	
	second-hand	from £75	
Boosey & Hawkes	B & H 400	£220	
	Besson 600	£350	ask for details
Paxman	Getzen Classic	£200	ask for details
	Bach Mercedes I	£300	

SUGGESTED LISTENING
Mozart: Requiem (*Tuba mirum* section)
Beethoven: 3 *Equali* for Trombone Quartet
Weber: Overture *Freischütz*
Wagner: Overture *Tannhäuser*
Stravinsky: *Pulcinella*
Rimsky-Korsakov: Trombone Concerto
Hindemith: Trombone Sonata
Milhaud: Trombone Concertino
Copland: *Rodeo*
Arnold: *Trombone Fantasy*
Bernstein: *Elegy for Mippy II*

Jazz: Tommy Dorsey, Robin Eubanks, J. J. Johnson, Jack Teagarden

SUGGESTED STUDY
A Tune A Day: *Trombone* (Chappell)
Cimera-Hovey Method for Trombone (Chappell)
Lafosse: *Méthode Complète* (in English) (Leduc)
Langey: *The Trombone* (Boosey & Hawkes)
Rubank Elementary Method for Trombone (Rubank)
Wastall: *Learn as you play: Trombone* (Boosey & Hawkes)
Wick: *Trombone Technique* (OUP)

POSTSCRIPT
Sir Thomas Beecham to over-taxed trombonist: 'Are you producing as much sound as possible from that antique drainage system you are applying to your face?'

The tuba is certainly the most intestinal of instruments, the very lower bowel of music.
PETER DE VRIES,
The Glory of the Hummingbird

Tuba

Popularity Rating: unavailable

Who is that faceless instrumentalist sitting next to the three Trombones? His features are entirely hidden behind an impressive mass of plumbing. It must be the Tuba player. Tuba, that is, to the orchestral world; in the Brass Band its name is B flat Bass or E flat Bass (see section on Band Instruments). To confuse you just a little more, there is also a Tenor Tuba, but its place is in the Brass Band, where it is called Euphonium.

Between 13 and 18 ft of metal tubing goes to produce this little monster. It is the lowest sounding of the brass family and, like the Horn and the Trumpet, but unlike the orchestral Trombone, it is fitted with valves. The tone production resembles that of the other brass instruments, and its astonishing range spans three octaves.

The Tuba, or Bass Tuba, is a non-transposing instrument, and the player reads his music in the bass clef.

It is a mere 170 years old. The prototypes were created by Wilhelm

Wieprecht, a bandmaster in the Prussian Dragoons. They were eagerly seized on by the military bands, but it took quite some time until symphony orchestras realized their potential. Now the Tuba occupies a permanent position, reinforcing its neighbours, the Trombones, and supplying a solid bass fundament to the orchestral texture.

An interesting offshoot was grafted on to the Tuba's family tree by Richard Wagner, when he designed the *Wagner Tuba*, recognizable by its oval shape and using a Horn mouthpiece. You can hear a whole shoal of them, sombre and majestic, at the beginning of the second scene of *Rheingold*, as they announce the *Walhall* theme.

Is the Tuba your instrument? Consider the following points:

1 It is expensive to buy, but may be available on loan, like its fellow leviathans, the Harp and the Double Bass.
2 Is your bedroom large enough to house a baby elephant?
3 How are you going to transport it?
4 Stop worrying about lung power: the Tuba needs less than the Trumpet.
5 Tuba players are wanted by orchestras as well as bands of all kinds. It is a prestigious instrument.
6 Technically, it is not too demanding, and its music tends to move at a leisurely pace.

Enquire from dealers and manufacturers (see Fact File II) about current prices of new and second-hand instruments, and about rental schemes. As a general guide, expect prices to start at about £650 for a new instrument, and from £400 for a second-hand one.

SUGGESTED LISTENING
Rimsky-Korsakov: *Sheherazade*
Mussorgsky (orch. Ravel): Bydlo, from *Pictures at an Exhibition*
Wagner: Overture *Meistersinger*
Vaughan Williams: Tuba Concerto
Bax: Symphony No. 2, slow movement
Hindemith: Tuba Sonata
Harvey: *Lightness and Weight*
Danny Kaye: 'Tubby the Tuba'

SUGGESTED STUDY
Arban: *First and Second Year Tuba Playing* (Fischer)
Bell: *Foundation to Tuba Playing* (Fischer)
Bernaud: *Méthode Complète* (in English) (Leduc)

Bevan: *The Tuba Family* (Faber)
Rubank Elementary Method: *Tuba* (Rubank)
Student Instrumental Course: *Tuba Student* (Belwin Mills)
Wastall: *Learn As You Play Tuba* (Boosey & Hawkes)

POSTSCRIPT
Sir Thomas Beecham to luckless Tuba player who has just produced an impressive long trill, unfortunately on the wrong note: 'Thank you very much. Now would you please pull the chain?'

Some day the Press will awake to the fact, already known abroad and to some few of us in England, that the living centre of music in Great Britain is not London but somewhere farther north.
EDWARD ELGAR

Band Instruments
Cornet – Flugelhorn – Tenor Horn – Baritone – Euphonium – Bass

Popularity Rating: unavailable

When Elgar spoke, in 1903, of *farther north*, he had Yorkshire and Lancashire in mind. For that is where ordinary folk had realized the thrill of making music in bands and in choirs. Brass Bands such as the Black Dyke Mills were sponsored, in the nineteenth century, by the mill owners who provided instruments, tuition and uniforms for their employees. Likewise, prudent employers initiated large choral enterprises, such as the Huddersfield Choral Society, which created musical experiences for countless amateurs and, over the years, for hundreds of thousands of listeners. Thus, music was allowed to grow naturally, in an unsophisticated manner, out of the hands, lips and throats of caring, committed men, women and their children.

The band instruments listed above find abundant employment in Brass Bands and Military Bands. The latter are also called Concert Bands or Wind Orchestras when their members are civilians. The following Table shows typical line-ups, though rather larger ensembles are also popular:

71

Brass Band	Military Band
1 Cornet in E flat	1 Flute/Piccolo
4 Cornets in B flat	1 Oboe
1 Flugelhorn	1 Clarinet in E flat
3 Tenor Horns	8 Clarinets in B flat
2 Baritones	1 Bassoon
3 Tenor Trombones	1 Alto Saxophone
1 Bass Trombone	1 Tenor Saxophone
1 Euphonium	2 French Horns
2 E flat Basses	6 Cornets (or Trumpets)
2 B flat Basses	2 Tenor Trombones
1 Side Drum	1 Bass Trombone
1 Bass Drum	1 Euphonium
1 Cymbals	1 E flat Bass
	1 B flat Bass
	1 String Bass (Double Bass)
	1 Bass Drum
	1 Cymbals

(It will be seen that the larger Military Band includes Woodwind as well as Brass instruments.)

Among the famous Brass Bands of today are the Morris Motors, Desford Colliery Dowty, Newham, Grimethorpe Colliery, and Brighouse & Rastrick Bands, as well as over 700 Salvation Army Bands. Well known Military Bands are the Household Cavalry, Royal Artillery, Grenadier Guards, Royal Marines, Royal Air Force, Regimental Bands and Metropolitan Police.

The enormous popularity of the non-orchestral brass instruments is based on two factors. They are easier to learn than their orchestral counterparts, and they lead to early participation in musical activities peculiar to the band world, with its festivals, competitions, indoor and outdoor concerts, parades, social events and touring.

The Cornet, developed in the early part of the nineteenth century, derives from the Posthorn. Its tone is rounder than that of the Trumpet with which it shares its playing technique. Berlioz used it in his *Symphonie Fantastique*, as did Bizet in the opera *Carmen*. The Cornet usually plays the same part in the band as does the Violin in the orchestra. The most accomplished Cornet player is nominated Solo Cornet, a position similar in scope and responsibility to that of the leader of the orchestra. Requiring less lung power than the Trumpet, the Cornet can be taken up by children not yet ten.

The Flugelhorn, like the Cornet, is pitched in B flat, while the Tenor Flugelhorn is in E flat. It has the same range as the Cornet, but its tone is richer, on account of its wider tube and bell. It dates back to the middle of the nineteenth century and is of German origin. Occasionally, the Flugelhorn appears in the symphony orchestra. Vaughan Williams admitted it to his Ninth Symphony, and Respighi employed it for his *Pines of Rome*.

The Tenor Horn, or E flat Horn, looks like a miniature Tuba, but is much easier to hold. It can be studied in a short time and is an ideal instrument for frustrated French Horn players who will adore the mellow sound of this cuddly instrument with its upward pointing bell.

The Baritone and Euphonium, pitched in B flat, play a similar role in the band to that of the Cello in the orchestra. Their tone is warm and substantial, and neither is particularly difficult to learn. Again, these instruments first appeared in Germany in the middle of the nineteenth century. They were quickly adopted by military bands, where they took the place of the less powerful Bassoon.

The Basses are the counterparts of the orchestral Tubas. The smaller one is pitched in E flat and the larger in B flat. With their bells pointing upwards, they are usually seated in front of the Percussion and just behind the Baritone and Euphonium.

One of those instruments is for you, if band life appeals to you, if you are set on a military music career, if you have connections with the band world, if you have not much time for practising but plenty for playing, if there is a band – and therefore teachers – in your neighbourhood, if the thought of fairly rapid results appeals to you, if you are gregarious by inclination, if you are solitary but would like to overcome your shyness, if you can see yourself playing while you march along, if you have a liking for ceremony, colour and uniforms.

Examples of current prices of instruments:

Firm	Instrument	Cost
	CORNET	
Paxman	Sonora	£125
Boosey & Hawkes	B & H 400 with case	£175
Myatt	Corton	£145
	second-hand	from £75
Lewington	Yamaha with case	£325
Vincent Bach	141 SP with case	£180

BAND INSTRUMENTS

Firm	Instrument	Cost
	FLUGELHORN	
Paxman	Lafleur	£130
Boosey & Hawkes	B & H 400 with case	£255
Myatt	Sonora	£190
	second-hand	from £165
Lewington	Yamaha with case	£450
Vincent Bach	144L with case	£195
	TENOR HORN	
Paxman	Weltklang	£220
Boosey & Hawkes	B & H 400 with case	£310
Myatt	Sonora	£265
	second-hand	from £135
Lewington	Parrot with case	£140
Vincent Bach	150L with case	£280
	BARITONE	
Paxman	Jupiter	£350
Boosey & Hawkes	B & H 400 with case	£360
Myatt	Corton	£310
	second-hand	from £250
Lewington	Hsinghai with case	£235
Vincent Bach	160L with case	£310
	EUPHONIUM	
Paxman	Lark	£230
Boosey & Hawkes	B & H 400 with case	£450
Myatt	Corton	£390
	second-hand	from £400
Lewington	Hsinghai with case	£235
Vincent Bach	170L with case	£400
	BASS	
Paxman		from £670
Boosey & Hawkes		from £655
Myatt		from £665
	second-hand	from £400
Lewington	with case	from £725

(Ask for details of rental terms.)

SUGGESTED LISTENING

Cornet
Berlioz: *L'Enfance du Christ*
Gounod: *Faust*
Wright: Concerto for B flat Cornet

Flugelhorn
Vaughan Williams: Ninth Symphony

Tenor Horn
Wood: Concertino for E flat Horn
Ball: *September Fantasy*

Euphonium
Young: Euphonium Sonata
Horovitz: Euphonium Concerto

Bass
(see Tuba in previous section)

Brass Band
Elgar: *The Severn Suite*
Holst: *A Moorside Suite*
Alwyn: *The Moor of Venice*
Vaughan Williams: *Variations for Brass Band*
Bantock: *Kubla Khan*
Rawsthorne: *Suite for Brass Band*

Military Band
Woolfenden: *Gallimaufry*
Bourgeois: *Symphony of Winds*
Jacob: *Old Wine in New Bottles*
Cruft: *Duke of Cambridge Suite*
Grainger: *A Lincolnshire Posy*
Holst: *Hammersmith*

Jazz
Big bands led by Count Basie, Duke Ellington, Gil Evans, Dizzy Gillespie

SUGGESTED STUDY

Cornet
Arban: *Cornet Method* (Cramer)
A Tune A Day: *Cornet* (Chappell)

Rubank Elementary Method for Cornet (Rubank)
The Cornet Primer (Wright & Round)

Flugelhorn
as for Trumpet and Cornet

Tenor Horn
A Tune A Day: *Tenor Horn* (Chappell)
Langey: *Tenor Horn Tutor* (Boosey & Hawkes)

Baritone
as for Trumpet (treble clef Baritone)
as for Euphonium (bass clef Baritone)

Euphonium
Langey: *Euphonium Tutor* (Boosey & Hawkes)

Bass
Hovey: *Elementary Method for Bass* (Rubank)
Skornicka: *Intermediate Method for Bass* (Rubank)

General
Belfrage: *Practice Methods for Brass Players* (Chester)
Ridgeon: *How Brass Players Do It* (Brass Wind)
Ridgeon: *The Physiology of Brass Playing* (Brass Wind)

For teachers and parents
Thompson: *Wind Bands and Brass Bands* (CUP)
Wright: *The Complete Bandmaster* (Pergamon)

POSTSCRIPT
The intrepid band . . .
Polish their mouthpieces and cough,
Then throw their shoulders back to play
A Pomeranian march. They're off!
And Sousa scares the tits away.

James Michie, 'Park Concert'

*A good drum does not
need hard striking.*
Japanese Proverb

Percussion

Popularity Rating: unavailable

For the moment forget about the *if only*. Look at this diary page instead:

Monday	Brass Band Rehearsal
Tuesday	Jazz Session
Wednesday	Orchestral Concert
Thursday	Pop Group Gig
Friday	Rock Session
Saturday	Dance Band Gig

This could be your diary, and those could be the six worlds of music with you as their monarch. *If only* you had the time. *If only* you could afford an orchestral Xylophone at £1200, a Drum Kit at £750, a set of Pedal Timpani at – but now we are getting into the realm of fantasy – well, if you insist, at £5000. *If only* you had a high-fidelity sense of rhythm. Three impediments to begin with. Since true musicians welcome obstacles as challenges to their initiative, they would soon find answers to the first two obstacles. By rearranging one's timetable it might be possible to fit in several playing sessions each week and still do justice to the homework. One could also start one's life as a percussionist by investing in a second-hand Snare Drum at £75. But all your ingenuity and enthusiasm will not assist you over the third hurdle, unless you have the makings of a rhythmical wizard. Test yourself.

Sit by a table and tap a steady *beat* with your left hand, while your right hand taps the *rhythm* of 'Oh the grand old Duke of York'.

Left Hand ♩ ♩ ♩ ♩ ♩ ♩ ♩ ♩ ♩ ♩ ♩ ♩ ♩ ♩ ♩ ♩

Right Hand ♫ ♪♪♪♪ ♩ ♪ ♪♪♪♪ ♩ ♪ ♪♪♪♪ ♪♪♪♪ ♪♪♪♪ ♩

Now change over and let your left hand tap the rhythm, with your right hand supplying the beat.

So far so good, but the real test is yet to come. Ask someone to assist. Start as before, one hand tapping time, the other tapping the rhythm. Then, at a moment of your helper's choosing, he calls 'Now'. This is your signal for switching instantaneously. Your right hand now does what your left hand had been doing, while your left hand takes over from your right. Repeat the process, until you are satisfied with your performance. Now proceed to the second part of the exercise. Bring in your feet, left foot duplicating left hand, right foot duplicating right hand. Again, obey your helper's command, this time hands and feet switching simultaneously from beat to rhythm and from rhythm to beat.

How are we doing? Impossible? In that case you have the author's leave to skip the rest of this section and proceed to the next. But if you have prospered, get ready for the third and final section, the *cross-over*. Left hand and right foot tap time, and right hand and left foot tap rhythm. Then switch when requested. Repeat this quite a few times and bring in other tunes as well. If you can keep cool control and if the whole business appeals to you, then you are a potential percussionist.

Trinity College of Music and Guildhall School of Music and Drama offer graded examinations in Percussion, specifying the following chief instruments:

Timpani (Kettledrum)
Snare Drum
Xylophone
Drum Kit

Obtain current details from both examination bodies.

As a timpanist you are in charge of two, three or even four Kettledrums which you play with sticks whose heads are made of felt, wood, cork or sponge. The material used depends on the effect you wish to produce. So does the intensity of the beat, the exact place where stick strikes playing surface, and the angle at which they meet. You will have to anticipate the conductor's beat and enter a tiny fraction of a second earlier than the other players, to allow the slower sound waves of your instrument to reach the audience together with the rest of the orchestra. You are also required to re-tune one or more drums, possibly several times during a performance, since the music may change key and demand new notes from the timpanist, or simply because the pitch has altered, due to changes in temperature and humidity. Re-tuning is done by putting your ear close to the playing surface, while turning the T-shaped handles clockwise or anti-clockwise and tapping the surface very quietly (nobody but you must hear!), until the desired pitch has been obtained. To make the timpanist's life less hectic, modern pedal Timpani (very expensive) allow the tension in the playing surface to be adjusted by raising or lowering a foot-operated mechanism. There is even a tuning gauge which indicates the pitch.

One of the hazards inherent in the construction of the Kettledrum is its sudden unbidden *singing*, when it responds to sounds in its vicinity. To calm your sensitive friend, you put a damping cloth on its playing surface. The surface, or *head*, is made of calf or goat skin which reacts to temperature variations, or plastic which does not.

It is essential for the learner to take some initial lessons from an expert. If you cannot find a teacher, contact the following:

Graham Hosker, Liaison Officer of the
National Association of Percussion Teachers,
4 Friston Green, Luton, Beds LU2 9SE

The same applies to intending players of the Snare Drum, the Xylophone or Vibraphone and the Drum Kit. Great perseverance is needed to master the drum roll. A practice pad eliminates the noise which otherwise might make your neighbours emigrate. The Xylophone, too, requires an accomplished roll, apart from deft crossing of hands and playing of two notes with one beater. Pianists and ex-pianists find this a particularly interesting instrument.

If you have scored well at our initial Duke-of-York Test, you may be the right person for the Drum Kit, for here the player must control several rhythm patterns at the same time, with both his hands and his feet. Ranged around him are Snare Drum and Bass Drum, the latter played by means of a pedal, one to three Toms (single-headed or double-headed drums), a Hi-Hat (pedal-operated Cymbals) and assorted percussion, such as Tambourine, Triangle, Woodblock and Whistle. Mounted on shining stands, this is the drummer's glittering empire or, more mundanely, his *kitchen*, where he finds ample scope for adventures in improvisation.

Whatever your choice of percussion instrument, you will always be in demand in orchestras, groups and bands. Your music is easy to read, which is just as well, for your mind and your limbs are on red alert from the first note to the last. The percussionist has nowhere to hide, with many eyes and ears fastened on his every move and error. It is a risky but glorious occupation.

For a special incentive, you might want to know about the Shell-LSO Music Scholarship for percussion players. This is, of course, for advanced students, but you may be able to attend the National Finals, usually held at London's Barbican Hall, as an onlooker. There, the motto, as always, is *inspiration – imitation – achievement*.

Examples of current prices:

Firm	Instrument	Cost
K.E.S.	Xylophone (non-orchestral)*	
	Soprano	£170
	Alto	£220
	Bass	£375
	Timpani (non-orchestral)*	
	Set of 3	£250
	Glockenspiel (non-orchestral)*	£60
	Snare Drum (non-orchestral)*	£135
	Xylophone (orchestral)	£1225
Premier	Drum Kit	£500
	Snare Drum	£235
	Marching Snare Drum	£195
	Bass Drum	£315
	Timpani	
	hand Set of 4	£1188
	pedal Set of 4	£2800
	Drummer's Practice Pad	£10
Vincent Bach	Drum Kit	£575
	Snare Drum	£215
	Bass Drum	£315
	Xylophone	£1575

(* Suzuki instruments, well made, suitable for learners.)

Addresses:
K.E.S. Music Service, 26 Elms Rd, Harrow Weald, Middx HA3 6BQ
Premier Percussion, Blaby Rd, Wigston, Leics LE8 2DF
Vincent Bach, Unit 23, Garrick Ind. Estate, Garrick Rd, London NW9
    6AQ

SUGGESTED LISTENING
Haydn: *Military Symphony*
Beethoven: Ninth Symphony (last movement)
Beethoven: *Wellington's Victory*
Rossini: Overture *William Tell*
Berlioz: *Symphonie Fantastique*
Berlioz: Requiem (*Tuba Mirum* section)
Verdi: Requiem (*Dies Irae* section)

Saint-Saëns: *Carnival of the Animals*
Shostakovich: Seventh Symphony
Bartók: *Music for Strings, Percussion and Celeste*
Bartók: Sonata for 2 Pianos and Percussion
Milhaud: Marimba Concerto
Messiaen: Symphony for Ten Percussionists
Orff: *Carmina Burana*
Britten: *The Young Person's Guide to the Orchestra*
Stockhausen: *Kontakte*
Reich: *Drumming* (Symphony)

Jazz drummers: *Art Blakey, Jo Jones, Philly Joe Jones, Max Roach*

SUGGESTED STUDY

Timpani
Baggers: *Method for Timpani* (Enoch)
Dupin: *Ear Training for the Kettledrummer* (Leduc)
Fink: *Studies for Timpani* (Schauer)
Whistler: *Elementary Method for Timpani* (Rubank)

Xylophone
Jolliff: *Intermediate Method for Xylophone* (Rubank)
Modern School for Xylophone (Kalmus)
Peterson: *Elementary Method for Xylophone* (Rubank)

Drums
Buggert: *Intermediate Method for Drums* (Rubank)
Fink: *Studies for Snare Drum* (Schauer)
The Premier Drum Book (Premier)
Savage: *The Art of the Drummer* (Music Sales)
Yoder: *Elementary Method for Drums* (Rubank)

Others
Blades: *Percussion Instruments and their History* (Faber)
Blades & Skinner: *Play Tuned Percussion* (Faber)

POSTSCRIPT
A percussion player asked Sir Malcolm Sargent,
'What do I have to know to play the Cymbals?'
'Nothing,' Sir Malcolm replied, 'just *when.*'

Singing

Swans sing before they die – 'twere no bad thing,
Did certain persons die before they sing.

SAMUEL TAYLOR COLERIDGE

Popularity Rating: 5/16

Singing is different. No tuition, at least not initially, no practising, no expense. After the Piano, Violin, Flute and Clarinet, more candidates choose singing for their examination subject than any of the other instruments. The voice unites the generations, for young children can compete on equal terms with adults of all ages who are eager to test their vocal skills by means of graded examinations.

What constitutes a good voice? One that makes people listen. One that pleases through its individual timbre and ease of tone production. One that can be remembered and recognized. One that approximates the sound of an instrument played by an expert, just as such an expert would like to think of his instrument rivalling the beauty of the human voice – Flute and Soprano, Viola and Alto, Trumpet and Tenor, Trombone and Bass. Above all, one that conveys the singer's own feelings.

The course from singing for pleasure to an examination and then to singing for further pleasure is almost self-selecting. School music teachers do not miss a promising voice, for they are needed in the choir where opportunities exist for descants, duets and solos. After some time, the choir director may suggest that some of the more prominent members should take a singing examination. It is quite possible to do well in such examinations without *individual* tuition. Most candidates of school age are able to absorb the necessary skills in the course of their musical activities at school. It is not advisable, anyway, to take lessons in voice production before the age of sixteen, seventeen or eighteen. When you are ready for specialized tuition, take the greatest care in locating a suitable teacher. There are some quite outstanding teachers in this field, but unfortunately far too many quacks are at large, who are eager to pass on their ignorance to the gullible, and to ruin their voices in the process. Always endeavour to listen to at least one of your prospective teacher's pupils.

The author asked several former members, now in their twenties, who used to belong to a renowned young ensemble in the Home Counties, to tell him of their life with the Choir. Amanda R. writes:

It was a totally new and somewhat overwhelming experience for me. I was the youngest member of the choir, and both anxious and keen to reach the high standard of the others. The vocal training which I received taught me how to use my voice to the best of its ability. I shall not forget the sheer pleasure of singing so many beautiful pieces with other talented people whose company I always enjoyed.

Jane G. writes:

I cannot remember a time when I didn't sing. There are two reasons why I started taking my voice seriously. The first was that my music teacher at school asked me why I didn't audition for the Borough Choir, as she thought my voice was good enough, and second, I had heard the songs they sung when my brother was in the same choir, and I thought theirs was the most varied and enjoyable repertoire of any choir I had heard before. The choir was my life between the ages of 11 and 19. I couldn't wait for the next rehearsal.

Provided a school or an adult choir is directed by someone knowledge-able and sympathetic, quite a few of its members could attempt graded examinations. Here is a summary of current requirements. *

	Associated Board Voice†	Associated Board Singing‡	Guildhall School of Music and Drama	Trinity College of Music	London College of Music
Grades	6–8	1–8	1–8	2–8	1–8
Songs	G 6–7:3 G 8:4	G 1–5:3 G 6–7:4 G 8:5 G 1–7: plus unacc. Folksong	G 1–4:2 G 5–8:3	3	3
Exercises	Yes	No	Yes G 5–7: plus Study	Yes	Yes
Sight-singing	Yes	Yes	Yes	Yes	Yes

* See pp. 117–22 for *instrumental* examination requirements.
† Intended for the mature and developed voice, the recommended minimum age being 16 for G 6, 17 for G 7 and 18 for G 8.
‡ Intended for singers whose voices are not as yet fully developed.

	Associated Board Voice	Associated Board Singing	Guildhall School of Music and Drama	Trinity College of Music	London College of Music
Aural	Yes	Yes	Yes	Yes	Yes
General musician- ship/ Viva voce	No	No	Yes	Yes	Yes
Written	Theory of Music or Practical Musician- ship G 5 must have been passed	G 6–8: Theory of Music or Practical Musician- ship G 5 must have been passed	G 8: Rudi- ments of Music G 5 must have been passed (for exemp- tions consult Syllabus)	G 6–8: Theory of Music or Musician- ship G 5 or higher must have been passed (for exemp- tions consult Syllabus)	G 6–8: Theory G 5 or higher must have been passed (for exemptions consult Syllabus)

What do the examiners expect from you? They may not all be expert singers themselves, but they enjoy a pleasant performance and are only too willing to acknowledge this. Such technical aspects as Exercises, Ear Tests and Sight Reading will be discussed in a later chapter. Let us here scrutinize the songs which you have prepared from a fairly wide list offered by your examination body.

In the examination room, place yourself by the side of the piano, preferably the treble end, in such a way that both accompanist and examiner are within your field of vision, but avoid singing straight *at* the examiner. Suppose you are about to launch into a song by Brahms, a composer much favoured by the various boards. You are of course familiar with his genial features. (You are *not*? You should be: composers are not faceless purveyors of melodies, they are your friends.) Picture Johannes Brahms smiling at you from the wall, somewhere above the examiner's head. Sing at Brahms and keep him smiling. Stand in a relaxed way, upright, and shift your weight slightly forward towards your toes. You will have learnt about efficient breathing, as opposed to shallow breathing. Make good use of it, to help your phrasing, to keep your tone steady and clear, and to project your voice even in quiet passages. Be understood: an otherwise fine performance can be marred by poor diction. Sing on the vowels, but make certain of the consonants. Discuss with your choir trainer and/or your singing teacher such aspects as *pure vowels* and *diphthongs*. Your intonation should not be a problem, provided your hearing is as keen as a musician's should be, and provided your breathing is well controlled.

We have mentioned posture, breathing, diction and intonation – all technical aspects which form the basis for your performance. You can and indeed you must become skilled in all these; but only when you are truly *involved* in your songs, will your singing be meaningful.

Let us suppose you are studying 'The vain suit' (*Vergebliches Ständchen*) by Brahms, which is on the list of songs for Grade 7 of the London College of Music. You are not required to sing this in the original German, though the Associated Board *requires* original language for Grades 7 and 8, Guildhall *prefers* it for Grades 6 to 8, while Trinity *requires* it for Grade 8 and keeps it *optional* for lower Grades.

Your first step: get hold of the German text. Then team up with an expert and a dictionary, and supply a word-by-word literal translation which is *not* meant to be sung. This gives you important indications of key words and phrases which the composer wishes to highlight, and which provide you with valuable clues for your performance. Write out the German text, line by line, with the English translation underneath each line, word by matching word, regardless of grammar or sense. Then write the English singer's words which appear in your printed music, by the side of your bilingual version. In some cases, the printed version is too awful to be of any use. It may distort the music by stressing words which the composer did not want to stress and vice versa, or it may simply be lamentable English which fails to do justice to the music. In that case try to improve upon it. Your team – teacher, family, friends – may regard this as a challenge to provide you with a workable version. Your final draft of Brahms' 'Vain suit' will look roughly like this:

'VERGEBLICHES STÄNDCHEN'
1 *Guten Abend, mein Schatz,,*
  Good Evening my treasure
  guten Abend, mein Kind.
  Good evening my child

'VAIN SUIT'
Good evening, my
sweetheart,
good evening, my dear.

Ich komm aus Lieb zu dir,
I come of love to you

ach, mach mir auf die Tür,
O make me open the door

mach mir auf, mach mir auf,
make me open make me open

mach mir auf die Tür.
make me open the door.

I come for love of you,

open the door, be true.

Let me in, let me in,

let me in and be true.

2 Mein' Tür ist verschlossen,
My door is locked

ich lass dich nicht ein.
I let you not in

Mutter, die rät mir klug,
Mother she advises me wisely

wärst du herein mit Fug,
were you inside with right
(= permission)

wär's mit mir vorbei,
were with me (all)over

wär's mit mir, wär's mit mir,
were with me were with me

wär's mit mir vorbei.
were with me (all)over.

My door will stay bolted,

you must not come in.

Mother has wit and skill:

if you would have your will,

I would be undone.

So she says, so she says,

I would be undone.

3 So kalt ist die Nacht,
So cold is the night

so eisig der Wind,
so icy the wind

dass mir das Herz erfriert,
that me the heart freezes

mein Lieb' erlöschen wird.
my love extinguish will

Öffne mir, mein Kind.
Open to me my child

Öffne mir, öffne mir,
Open to me open to me

öffne mir, mein Kind.
open to me my child

So cold is the night,

so icy the wind.

My heart will freeze to you,

my love will perish too.

Open up, my love!

Open up, open up,

let me in, my love!

4 Löschet dein Lieb',
Extinguished your love

If you are so wayward,

lass sie löschen nur.
let it extinguished just
Löschet sie immerzu,
Extinguished it all the time,
geh heim zu Bett, zur Ruh.
go home to bed to sleep
Gute Nacht, mein Knab'!
Good night my boy
Gute Nacht, gute Nacht,
Good night good night
gute Nacht, mein Knab'!
good night my boy.

be on your way, my lad.

Your love is chilled and dead,

go home and go to bed.

So good night, my lad.

So good night, so good night,

so good night, my lad.

For your next step, reduce each verse to its essentials, by paraphrasing the poetry into unembroidered prose, perhaps like this:

1 I am on my way to my sweetheart. Though it's late, I'm sure she will let me come in.
2 What is that she is saying? Her mother has advised her to keep me out? What? She says she would be undone if I came in?
3 I will plead harder. 'Now look here, love. It's bitterly cold. You don't want me to freeze to death? For if you do, my love for you may freeze too.'
4 'If your love can freeze, so be it. I thought you really cared for me. Ah well. Go home then, to your own bed. And good night to you!'

Now that we have established what the song is about, you can convey its meaning and its atmosphere to an audience.

This procedure of creating a blueprint of your song material will be equally useful for the other chosen songs. Steep yourself in their music, in their meaning. Once you are truly involved, you can involve your listeners, including your examiner. Your listeners will thank you with their applause, the examiner with marks galore, and the composer with a cordial smile from his elevated position on the wall of the examination room.

For your information, here is a breakdown of marks awarded by the examining bodies:

	AB Voice	AB Singing	G 1–4	5–8	T	L
Songs	90	111	54	42	60	15
Exercises Studies	21	–	18	30	15	
Sight-singing	21	21	9	9	10	10
Aural	18	18	10	10	10	8
Viva Voce/ General Musicianship	–	–	9	9	5	7
	150	150	100	100	100	100

100 = Pass	66 = Pass	65 = Pass	65 = Pass
120 = Merit	75 = Merit	75 = Merit	75 = First Cla
130 = Distinction	85 = Honours	85 = Honours	85 = Honour

A cautionary word. Should you elect to sing part of your programme in the original language, be it German, French or Italian, do take advice from someone who knows, preferably a native speaker of your chosen language. In his capacity as an examiner, the author has on several occasions been unable to decide in what language a particular candidate had been singing. There are many ways of mispronouncing a foreign word, but only one way to pronounce it correctly. Find it. For example, the German *Liebeslied*, song of love, is pronounced *leebisleet*. An unsuspecting candidate who had to sing a piece in which this word occurred at a dramatic moment pronounced it *lighbislight*, which unfortunately in German is stomach ache.

Finally, secure the sympathetic services of a skilful accompanist with whom to rehearse your programme and who will play for your examination. Good accompanists (see Gerald Moore's superb book, *The Unashamed Accompanist*) provide far more than the written notes. They establish the mood of each song or aria in the introductory bars, thus putting you (and the examiner) in the right frame of mind. They will breathe with you, creating opportunities for an extra intake of air when necessary, helping with phrasing and dynamics, and supporting your intonation in cases of emergency. The accompanist is the foremost member of your support team.

When you have studied your examination pieces, find out whether any of them have been recorded (local music shop and public library will help), not with the object of imitating the artists, but in order to compare your performance with theirs. Reject whatever does not suit you, and accept or modify details which strike you as relevant. A good model is one that leads you to realizing your own potential. With that in mind, study style and tone production of some particularly accomplished singers and choirs. You might like to listen to any of the following:

Soprano	Margaret Price – Elisabeth Grümmer
Alto	Janet Baker – Kathleen Ferrier
Tenor	Fritz Wunderlich – Peter Pears
Baritone	Dietrich Fischer-Dieskau – Olaf Bär
Bass	Kurt Moll – Robert Lloyd
Boy Soprano	Aled Jones – Nicholas Sillito
Choirs	Tölzer Knaben – King's Singers – Monteverdi Choir

SUGGESTED STUDY
Echols: *How to Read Music, a Handbook for Singers* (Elkin)
Fuchs: *The Art of Singing* (Calder)
Hewitt: *How To Sing* (Elm Tree)
Howe: *Practical Principles of Voice Production* (Novello)
Koster: *The Commonsense of Singing* (Thames)
Manén: *The Art of Singing* (Faber)
Marshall: *The Singer's Manual of English Diction* (Schirmer)
Odon: *The Singer's Manual of German and French Diction* (Schirmer)
Reid: *The Free Voice* (Elkin)
Rose: *The Singer and the Voice* (Scolar Press)
Schwarzkopf: *On and Off the Record* (Faber)
Slater: *Vocal Physiology and the Teaching of Singing* (Ashdown)

POSTSCRIPT
'It is a knowledge easely taught, and quickly learned, where there is a good Master, and an apt Scoller.

The exercise of singing is delightfull to Nature, and good to preserve the health of man.

It doth strengthen all parts of the brest, and open the pipes.

It is the best meanes to procure a perfect pronunciation, and to make a good Orator.

There is not any Musicke of Instruments whatsoever, comparable to that which is made of the voyces of Men, where the voyces are good, and the same well sorted and ordered.

Since singing is so good a thing
I wish all men would learne to sing.'

William Byrd, 'Reasons briefely set down
to perswade every one to learn to singe'

2 CHOOSING YOUR TEACHER

Teachers are by far the most
valuable members of
society.

YEHUDI MENUHIN

This chapter scrutinizes teachers, parents and students. It indicates how to secure high-quality tuition. It shows parents how to cooperate with the teacher. But this is an enquiry, not an inquisition.

Good teachers are the salt of the earth. Bad teachers should be shunned like the plague.

A bad teacher is always overpaid. A good teacher is never paid enough.

Some favourite words of a good teacher are *enthusiasm*, *discovery*, *sympathy*. Some favourite words of a bad teacher are *authority*, *routine*, *end of lesson*.

In his forty years as a music adviser, teacher, parent and examiner, the author has been thrilled when witnessing the fruits of inspired teaching, and sickened by the havoc wrought by ignorant, insensitive and bogus 'teachers'.

The good teacher is in love with music and knows how to inspire his or her pupils. The bad teacher is not and does not.

Before turning the spotlight on the three categories of teachers – the excellent, the mediocre and the appalling – we must grapple with that incubus, the Personal Pronoun. Do we really wish to refer to teachers and pupils, throughout this and all subsequent chapters, as *he or she*? Or shall we simplify matters by calling teachers *she* and pupils *he*? Thus we save unnecessary repetitions, while safeguarding both male and female claims to equality. Male teachers will understand, and female pupils, I trust, will forgive.

Happily, the hordes of inept teachers are balanced by an ever-growing contingent of experts. The good teacher sets out to form a personal relationship with her pupils. She takes a genuine interest in their lives, and she is not above granting them periodic glimpses into hers. She values each pupil for his own sake, and she is skilled in recognizing his musical potential. She regards her lessons as a dialogue between partners, and she is prepared to profit from her pupils' endeavours. Basil Tchaikov, the renowned clarinettist, put this point very neatly when, interviewed by the editor of *Music Teacher* magazine (June 1987), he said, 'I truly believe that a lesson in which the teacher does not feel he or she has learnt something isn't a very good lesson.'

The good teacher's music studio is her manifesto. It is well organized and bright, its piano is regularly tuned, the piano stool adjustable (sitting on telephone directories tends to lose its attraction for small customers after a few minutes) and wide enough to allow four-handed playing. The adjustable music stand is solid and reliable, and a few pictures and flowers will do their best. A mascot (teddy bear or suchlike) is at hand for the very young. There will be a waiting area, with the toilet not too far away. The lessons are punctual, for the expert teacher knows that Joanne's extra minutes are Colin's loss. She maintains brief lesson notes which help her in monitoring her pupils' progress. She liaises with her students' parents, enlisting their support and discussing problems well before they get out of hand.

The expert teacher arranges informal concerts, when *all* pupils play to their invited families, either in groups or on their own; all items are short and well within each player's capacity. She is level-headed on music examinations. She will neither insist that such an examination be taken, nor will she yield to unreasonable demands. She will not enter her pupils for one grade after another, thus allowing the choice of music to be dictated by the examination syllabus and not, as it should be, by her own counsel and her students' inclinations. But she may well advise on the desirability of periodic examinations, such as grades 1, 3, 5, 7 and 8, thus providing pupils, parents and herself with occasional external assessments, while at the same time affording her students the stimulus of performing at their own top level. Under no circumstances will she ever misread the examination syllabus and teach her unsuspecting pupils the wrong music. On the other hand, she will be familiar with *all* examination bodies, such as the Associated Board of the Royal Schools of Music, the Trinity College of Music, the Guildhall School of Music and Drama and the London College of Music, and she will be able to match each individual student's level of attainment with the most suitable examination syllabus. Since knowledge of musical theory and aural perception are essential parts of the graded examinations, she will either provide this tuition herself, or she will advise on how to obtain it.

The expert teacher is able to contradict the adage that *he who knows, does; he who doesn't, teaches*, for she frequently reinforces her tuition by demonstrating. She can also enlist the influential power of 'model' performers, by means of tape or disc. For example, cellists might be guided and inspired by listening to Rostropovich, pianists by Brendel, flautists by Bennett, guitarists by Bream, trombonists by Hext, horn players by Tuckwell, sopranos by Margaret Price, and young voices by soloists from the Vienna Boys' Choir. The expert teacher, whatever her chosen instrument, can accompany her string, woodwind, brass or singing students on the piano. She will play sensitively, providing the necessary support without being dominant, and she will *not* sit with her back to the student, even if that necessitates turning the piano around. She keeps herself up to date with recently published teaching material and with developments in her field, which she finds discussed in the music journal to which she subscribes and at meetings of the professional organization to which she belongs. She is well informed about such physical aspects of instrumental and vocal tuition as Posture and Relaxation, and she knows how to correct the former and promote the latter.

Our dedicated teacher has made a special study of the art of practising, and she is able to explain the reasons for regular, informed practice; she will also demonstrate the technique of the practising process, and she is resourceful in enlisting the parents' cooperation in this vital field. The expert teacher can frequently be seen in the auditorium of concert halls, and as she listens to Itzakh Perlman playing Beethoven's *Spring Sonata*, she will feel doubly elated when she spots one of her pupils in the hall. It is at such moments that the magic of music grips them both, as it allots them places in their cultural heritage – the composer who inspires the performer who inspires the teacher who inspires her pupil.

Not a great deal of inspiration can be expected from another category of teachers: the middling, the brave average. Their musical horizons may be limited, but they will be able to provide their pupils with a fairly proficient playing technique. The student's team members – family, friends, school – will often compensate for the teacher's limitations by providing added stimulus and support. They can create opportunities for listening experiences at live concerts and at home, and for contact with other students with a view to joint music making. The best that can be said of the average teacher is that her averageness is her strength: she is generally reliable, predictable in her actions and reactions, and she will not do much harm. One of the characteristics of this category is its impermanence. Many of its members may become expert teachers in the course of time, while others – often through sheer boredom or ill health – drift towards the bottom of their profession.

It is not entirely surprising that there are so many poor music teachers at large. In their annual report (21 July 1987), Her Majesty's inspectors of schools suggest that one third of all school teachers in England are below average. It is a fair assumption – borne out, alas, by experience – that a similar ratio applies to teachers of music, both in schools and in the home. The report criticizes the *below average* teachers for expecting too little of their pupils, for failing to stimulate their interest, for inefficient planning and for 'poor perception of their pupils' educational needs'.

While it is up to our training establishments, music colleges and universities to improve this sorry state of affairs, we must guard against securing the services of a member of this army of lame ducks. Since that fowl is spotted by its strut, the species can be avoided.

The incompetent teacher has a chaotic studio. She asks her pupils, 'Where did we stop last week?', because she failed to make a note. Her lessons begin late and end early, or vice versa. She answers the phone and the doorbell during her lessons. She attends to the mail and the washing machine. Sometimes she smokes, sometimes she dresses sloppily. Often she regrets the time when she turned to teaching, when she had not quite made it as a performer, due to adverse circumstances – her euphemism for lack of talent. She seldom visits concerts, she reads no musical journals, she does not belong to any professional organization which might help her to widen her horizon. She does not, cannot, will not share her pupils' interests, being a stranger to this year's TV soap operas, to the world of computers, to current dress fashion, to pop groups and their hits, and to the football league tables.

When the bad teacher says, 'I do not undertake aural training or theory', she means, 'I don't know how to do it.' When her pupils ask her why they should practise scales, she fails to provide a satisfactory explanation. She will teach a piece of music in two separate stages. First the notes, week after week, until they are as correct as they will ever be. Then she announces, 'Next week we shall put in the expression,' without suspecting that a piece which has been allowed to be played mechanically has long lost any appeal to the player and will remain a burdensome trifle ever after. Thus, the incompetent teacher is able to kill the joy of making music with deadly rapidity. If she is a violinist, she will also cheerfully teach the Cello and the Double Bass, and if she is a clarinettist, she will inflict her non-specialist knowledge and the wrong embouchure upon prospective flautists, oboists and bassoonists.

The teacher to avoid puts her pupils through the graded examinations, intending to cover the lot, from Grade 1 to Grade 8, but seldom progressing beyond the early stages. She advertises *her* successes but keeps quiet about *their* failures. She is apt to prepare the wrong pieces, having misread the instructions or worked on an outdated syllabus.

When she accompanies her string pupils in the examination room, she will play very loudly indeed, confident that the examiner will then not spot their mistakes. If she does not herself accompany, she is liable to be vague over the examination arrangements. Has her pupil's father booked the accompanist and has he told him *when* to turn up and *where*? Or will the accompanist arrive, as he so often does, late and out of breath, eroding the candidate's confidence and the examiner's sweet nature, especially since he has brought the wrong music along? Frequently she will send the examiner a note, via the candidate, saying (I quote):

Dear Examiner,
    Eunice is taking her Grade 2 today. I write to ask for your indulgence. She has not practised very hard these last three years, ever since she took Grade 1, but her father has promised her a bicycle if she passes. She will then have an extra ten minutes each week, since she will be able to cycle to my home.
    Yours hopefully . . .

When the results arrive, she will complain to the examination board: the examiner was prejudiced/tone-deaf/intimidating/incompetent.

Two cautionary tales from the author's experience shall round off this dismal section. The first concerns an elderly lady violinist whose teacher had entered her for a Grade 6 examination. This is one of the higher grades and requires a respectable standard of performance. Unfortunately, the candidate was unable to play a single note in tune. None of her pieces progressed beyond the first few bars, while her grip of the instrument and the bow was totally wrong. She scored a blank on her aural tests, and her sight reading was faulty throughout. It can only be assumed that the lady's teacher was lacking in competence and candour – an assumption which was sadly confirmed a year later when, by an odd chance, candidate and examiner met for a second time. Again, she had been misled by her teacher to attempt Grade 6. Again, her performance would not have passed a very much lower grade. The examiner was left to reflect on the frustration, the amount of time and, presumably, of money and good will, all spent in the vain pursuit of an illusion.

The second tale is quickly told. When the examiner entered the waiting room to greet the assembled candidates for the afternoon session, he sensed an atmosphere of gloom and unnatural quiet. Seven boys and girls and their teacher were silently facing each other, expressionless and immobile. After the examiner had tried to cheer them all up, the teacher whispered in his ear, proudly and in explanation, 'All my pupils hate me!'

If anything mentioned so far sounds exaggerated or incredible, let the reader be assured that, alas, every incident, every example, every character trait is true to its wretched life.

Strangely, but fortunately, there exists still another category. It is inhabited by the eccentric, the capricious, the whimsical, the crotchety, the maverick. Her studio and her timetable are a mess, she mislays her music, she tricks out her lessons with tales from her youth, her piano is as moribund as her pitiful parrot, and all her pupils worship her. For her sake they will practise until it hurts. For her sake they put up with discomfort and irregularity. They love music, because they love her.

Blessed be the non-conformists.

It should be pointed out at this stage that whenever this book refers to *pupils*, that term covers the whole age and ability range, from infant beginner to adult student. It should also be borne in mind that the advice offered within these pages applies as much to instrumental as to singing students.

Whatever your age, whatever your musical pursuit, you will need a teacher. No book, no correspondence course, no video tutor can replace an efficient teacher. It is essential, especially for the beginner, to avail himself of his teacher's vigilance, expertise and individually tailored advice. The choice of the right teacher, therefore, is of utmost importance. It is regrettable that many parents give no more thought to choosing a music teacher than they would give to choosing a television set. Yet, the wrong teacher can spoil a student's appetite for music for the rest of his life, while the right one intensifies it. Much time, patience and ingenuity is needed for locating your teacher. How will you find her? Here are fifteen practical suggestions. Try any combination of these.

1 Make personal enquiries of families of music students in your neighbourhood. You can spot them on a warm day, when the windows are open, and you will recognize them in the streets by their instrument cases. Few parents will object to your questions, and you might gather some useful information from both satisfied and disgruntled customers. At this stage it is best to collect names and addresses of prospective teachers, no matter whether they are recommended or not. Later you will have to decide which teachers to approach and which to discount. Advice on this crucial choice can be found on pp. 100–107.

2 The Incorporated Society of Musicians (ISM) issues a *Register of Professional Private Music Teachers* which can be consulted in the reference section of your public library. The Register lists teachers, their addresses and telephone numbers, together with their qualifications, grouped according to their instruments and then again alphabetically.

The countries covered are England, Wales, Scotland, Northern Ireland and the Channel Islands, but there are also a few overseas entries. Not many readers will be familiar with the abbreviations of the great number of degrees and diplomas which denote their holders' qualifications. The list of Music Degrees and Diplomas in Fact File IV may be found helpful.

3 Contact the Musicians' Union and ask for particulars of teachers in your area:

Musicians' Union, 60–62 Clapham Rd,
London SW9 0JJ (Tel. 01 582 5566)

4 There are several Associations for performers and teachers of specific instruments. Ask their secretaries to put you in touch with possible teachers of your instrument:

Piano   European Piano Teachers' Association,
             28 Emperor's Gate, London SW7 4HS
             (Tel. 01 373 7307)

Harpsichord Glasgow Harpsichord Society,
             14 Sandend Rd, Glasgow G53 7DG (Tel.
             041 882 6127)

Organ   British Institute of Organ Studies,
             Dept. of Music, University of Reading, Berks. RG1 5JE
             (Tel. 0734 873583)

             Cathedral Organists' Association,
             Royal School of Church Music, Addington Palace,
             Croydon CR9 5AD (Tel. 01 654 7676)

             City of London Society of Organists,
             Hill House, 17 Hans Place, London SW1X 0EP
             (Tel. 01 589 5925)

             Organ Club,
             10 Roxburgh Court, 69 Melrose Rd,
             London SW18 1PG (Tel. 01 870 7784)

             Royal College of Organists,
             Kensington Gore, London SW7 2QS (Tel.
             01 589 1765)

             Ulster Society of Organists and Choirmasters,
             1b Beverley Hills, Bangor, N.I., BT20 4NA
             (Tel. 0247 465222)

97

Singing	Association of Teachers of Singing, 241 Maldon Rd, Colchester, Essex CO3 3BQ (Tel. 0206 570 667)
Harp	United Kingdom Harp Association, 39 Villiers Close, Surbiton, Surrey, KT5 8DN (Tel. 01 390 2634)
Strings	European String Teachers' Association, 5 Neville Ave, New Malden, Surrey, KT3 4SN (Tel. 01 942 8191)
Woodwind	Association of Woodwind Teachers, 100 Common Rd, Chatham, Kent, ME5 9RG
	British Flute Society, 65 Marlborough Place, London NW8 0PT (Tel. 01 624 8707)
	Clarinet and Saxophone Society of Great Britain, 24c Wellwood Rd, Goodmayes, Essex, IG3 8TR
	Dolmetsch Foundation, High Pines, Wood Rd, Hindhead, Surrey, GU26 6PT (Tel. 042873 4895)
Brass	British Horn Society, 116 Long Acre, London WC2E 9PA (Tel. 01 240 3642)
	National Association for Brass Teachers in Education, 90 Allesley Old Rd, Coventry CV5 8DF (Tel. 0203 418868)
Band Instruments	British Federation of Brass Bands, 21 Woulds Court, Moira, Burton on Trent, Staffs, DE12 6HB (Tel. 0530 414663)
	British Association of Symphonic Bands and Wind Ensembles, Silver Birches, Bentinck Rd, Altrincham, Ches., WA14 2BP (Tel. 061 928 8354)
Percussion	National Association of Percussion Teachers, 138 Upperthorpe, Walkley, Sheffield, S6 3NF

5 There are numerous amateur orchestras in all areas of the country. Check the local paper and public libraries for addresses of their secretaries, and find out whether any of their members are available for tuition.

6 Many professional instrumentalists also teach. Approach the secretaries of your nearest professional orchestras. You find their names and addresses, under *Symphony and Chamber Orchestras*, in:

British Music Yearbook,
Rhinegold Publications Ltd,
241 Shaftesbury Ave, London WC2H 8EH

7 For teachers of brass and brass band instruments, try Army, Military and Brass Bands, also listed in the above publication. Some first-rate tutors can be found in those institutions. Also, do not overlook your local amateur band, some of whose members may well be suitable teachers.

8 Your local Amateur Operatic Society (particulars via public library) probably uses several proficient instrumentalists as well as singers, who may be available to teach.

9 Look in the Yellow Pages, under *Music Tuition*.

10 Search your local press for advertisements by music teachers and for reports of their examination successes.

11 Seek advice from the organists and choirmasters of the churches in your neighbourhood.

12 Visit the local music shop. Its manager will have valuable connections in the teaching profession.

13 Music periodicals will yield much useful information. Consult the following:

British Music Education Yearbook	*Music and Musicians*
British Music Yearbook	*Music Teacher*
Clarinet and Saxophone	*Opera*
Classical Guitar	*Organ*
Classical Music	*Organists' Review*
Guitarist	*Organist Today*
Guitar Player	*Piano Journal*
Keyboard Player	*Recorder Magazine*
Musical Opinion	*The Recorder*
Musical Times	*The Strad*

For publishers' addresses see *British Music Yearbook*.

14 This is the author's favourite method of discovering teachers of instrumental and vocal music. Ask your local public library for details of music festivals in your area, then visit as many sessions as you possibly can. Amidst the profusion of young and mature talent, you will spot a few performers whose musical sensitivity and technical prowess will please you. Approach them or their escorts and ask for their teachers' names. Frequently you will find the teachers present in the hall. Observe their relationship with their pupils. Is it stiff and remote, or do their charges huddle round them, sparkling and relaxed? Here is your opportunity to see and hear the fruits of loving and expert tuition or of the other kind.

15 If you are still searching, avail yourself of the exhaustive list in Fact File V, which contains details of local education authorities' Music Advisers, County Music Advisers, Schools specializing in Music, Youth Orchestras, Colleges of Further Education, Teacher Training Establishments, Music Colleges and Universities. We have dispensed with addresses and names, since these are liable to change. Instead, it is suggested that you phone the establishments in your area, with a view to obtaining details of members of staff and advanced students who are prepared and qualified to teach the instrument of your choice. Do not be daunted by the length of the list, but target your search on your home county. Good hunting!

If you have adapted the search procedure to your needs, you will by now have compiled names and addresses of *possible* teachers. Your next step will result in turning this list into a much shorter one of *likely* teachers. It is a crucial step to take. It requires initiative, patience and ingenuity.

First, obtain an interview. If possible, arrange to visit the teacher at her home. This will provide you with a glimpse of her studio and its milieu. Respect the teacher's busy schedule and avoid digressions. Be friendly and open, and state at the outset that the questions you are going to ask are intended to help all three parties – teacher, pupil and parents – to decide whether they are made for one another. Your son or daughter should not be present at this fact-finding interview. You will be wise to be well prepared. It is essential for the teacher to feel that you have not come as a snooper but as a well disposed emissary.

You may be handed a prospectus which sets out, among other things, the tuition fees and other matters to be mutually agreed. In the absence of a prospectus, ask for the conditions of tuition; enquire about the duration of a lesson; about how many lessons there are in a term, and how many terms in a year; ask whether they coincide approximately with school terms or not, and find out what happens if either side misses or cancels a lesson. This will lead you to a question which should determine the further course of your discussion:

Are you prepared to regard the first five lessons as a mutual trial period?

The author is convinced that it is necessary for all parties concerned to find out whether they are likely to form a fruitful relationship. If after a half term's tuition either side has reservations about this, it is in everybody's interest to part company. If the prospective teacher will not agree to a mutual trial term, you may feel that this is the moment to thank her and terminate the interview. If, however, you are still in accord with each other, proceed to the following key questions. It is unnecessary and indeed undesirable for you to trespass on the teacher's time and forbearance by asking the whole set of questions. Choose those which you think most relevant. The replies should enable you to form an opinion of the teacher's personality and professional outlook, and to determine whether you should proceed further. Impress upon the teacher that at the end of your question period you would be happy for her to reverse the process.

1 Please tell me about your teaching experience.

Do not be put off by even a total absence of experience. Everybody has to start somewhere, and a fresh, unjaded mind can be a great asset.

2 Would you object to my presence at one of the first lessons?

If the teacher is prepared to grant your wish, this should be regarded as a privilege, since it is a somewhat unusual request. Do show your appreciation. You might explain that such personal, though passive involvement will help you to support and reinforce some tuition points, in a non-technical manner, between lessons. On the other hand, if the teacher objects, this should not be held against her. She may have very valid reasons for saying no.

3 What are your views on graded examinations?

Beware a rigid attitude on the teacher's part. Running the whole course of examinations, from the first to the final grade, can be soul-destroying, while rejecting examinations altogether deprives the student of a valuable experience. If the reply is positive, find out whether the teacher is familiar with the differences between the various syllabuses.

101

4 Which examination board do you prefer and why?

The teacher ought to be aware of, say, the Associated Board, the Trinity College and the Guildhall School.

5 Do you undertake aural training and theory instruction?

If the teacher is in favour of periodic examinations, this extra tuition must be provided, possibly in the form of additional lessons given by the teacher or someone she recommends, or as an integral part of the instrumental or vocal instruction. Both aural training and a knowledge of musical theory, i.e. the rudiments of music, are an essential part of every music student's training. Without them there will be scant technical progress, and the student's musical perception and appreciation will be found wanting.

6 What are your guidelines on practising?

The student who has been motivated to practise regularly, concentratedly and effectively will generally make far greater progress than the one who has not. This vital accomplishment will be discussed at some length in chapter four, and the prospective teacher's views should provide evidence that she has given serious thought to this aspect of music teaching.

7 Do you enter your students for music festivals?

As in the case of graded examinations, the occasional participation in a festival – preferably the non-competitive kind – constitutes a joyful event, when students can listen to their colleagues, while also enjoying the opportunity of seeing and hearing instruments other than their own.

8 How do you like your pupils' parents to be involved?

Most good teachers expect their students' parents to provide a judicious mixture of encouragement and supervision. If she appears indifferent, beware.

9 I would like to know more about my child's instrument. Can you recommend any books for me to study?

If the answer is negative, beware even more. A teacher's tools of the trade should be at her fingertips and on the tip of her tongue.

10 Do you issue periodical progress reports?

Here, a negative reply does not indicate a negative attitude. A teacher can be brilliant without ever writing a single word about the results of her brilliant tuition. However, parents will (or should) welcome the occasional written or oral communication on their children's progress.

11 Do your pupils have assignment notebooks?

Many expert teachers regard such a notebook as an essential, being far more effective than the weekly scribble in the student's printed music which can so easily get out of hand. It also provides a means of communication with parents. The older the student, the less need for a notebook.

12 Do you allow your more advanced pupils to play in their school orchestras, if asked?

Quite a few excellent teachers are strongly against their students' being involved in musical activities over which they have no control and which might expose the learner to forms of tuition, however incidental, which could conflict with the teacher's way of coaching. This is misguided. So much joy can be found, at any level, in making music with others, that the remote risk of the student's playing technique being adversely affected is worth taking. It is always possible and indeed desirable for the teacher to bring her fears to the attention of the conductor of the school ensemble in question. He, too, is a member of the student's team and will be glad to cooperate. The author recalls an occasion when a choirmaster – one of the finest in the country – was told by the singing teacher of one of his members that Nicholas was no longer permitted to attend choir rehearsals. Why? 'Because it spoils his voice.'

13 Do you arrange occasional students' get-togethers?

Informal students' recitals, visits to concerts and other outings are always to be welcomed. They are the logical outcome of a happy teacher-pupil relationship.

14 Assuming that it would be helpful for my son to listen to performers on the instrument of his choice, whom do you recommend?

The expert teacher is familiar with the names of many players of her instrument, regardless of her views on their suitability as 'models'. If no names are forthcoming, beware.

At the end of the interview you should acquaint the teacher with your child's present state of musical development. Can he read notation? Has he got a good ear? Has he had previous tuition? If you want the teacher to accept your child for tuition, assure her of your full cooperation (and mean it). If you are a mature student, you will of course be negotiating on your own behalf and will have re-phrased your questions accordingly. Whether parent or adult student, the teacher's personality, her professional attitude, her candour, the state of her studio, will all help you in forecasting the kind of relationship which the prospective pupil is likely to form with this particular teacher.

You must now be prepared to face the teacher's questions, and to answer them candidly. To help her appraise the chances for a successful partnership, the teacher should try to obtain answers to any or all of the following:

1 Does your child want to take lessons or is it your own wish?

For a child to be pushed or cajoled into learning to play a particular instrument is not an auspicious beginning. An expert teacher may well decline to teach under such circumstances.

2 Are you willing and able to provide a reasonable instrument, as well as the necessary music and accessories?

While it is often possible to hire an instrument (see previous chapter), accessories (music stands, bows, mutes, cleaning materials etc) and printed music can be quite costly. The question merits careful consideration.

3 Is there a suitable room for your child to practise?

The teacher will advise you that such a room must be solely at the child's disposal while he is practising. She may not object to one or both parents' presence, provided this is for the exclusive purpose of listening.

4 Are you prepared to tolerate daily practice?

This question may sound odd, but the teacher has valid reasons for asking it. She may have encountered situations where a member of the household is on night shift and finds the noise unappealing, or where snide remarks by members of the family had made the student lose heart. Remember that the initial efforts, especially those of a violinist and a clarinettist, can be somewhat distressing to anyone within earshot. The best way to shorten that tedious period is praise, constant encouragement and cotton wool.

5 Will you keep an eye on your child's progress by asking him to play for you?

Few children find satisfaction in practising their music for its own sake. They need an audience, and you must provide it.

6 Are you going to ask me to teach your child any particular music of your choice?

Concede the point and promise not to. It is a case of *teacher knows best*. There may be exceptions, of course, where parents' wishes and teacher's judgement coincide, but do not rely on it.

7 What other activities, apart from school work, make their demands on your child's time?

It is not fair on either teacher or pupil to commence lessons, while all available time is already taken up by football, hockey, guides, computers and cycling. The whole situation needs to be discussed with the prospective student. Only you, your child and his school teachers will know whether there is sufficient ungrudged leisure time for a new, demanding pursuit.

8 Will you ensure your child's regular and punctual attendance?

If you can visualize – even at the back of your mind – circumstances which justify cancelling a lesson, please reconsider. Illness is an excuse, hardly anything else is. Certainly not auntie's birthday, the pantomime or the family outing. The more fastidious you are in this matter, the greater the prestige which the lessons will acquire in your child's estimation.

9 Do you wish me to teach at your home?

Not all teachers will consider this. If your circumstances make such an arrangement desirable, explain them and be prepared to pay a higher fee; the teacher loses time, i.e. revenue, travelling to and fro, and has to carry her teaching material. If she agrees, endeavour to create teaching conditions at your home which match those which you would expect at the teacher's.

10 Will you agree to your child taking periodic graded examinations?

Since you are a reader of this book, you will. So be prepared for additional cost in the shape of entrance fees, examination music and possibly extra fees for aural training and theory.

Your lengthy search is over: you may have found the ideal teacher, and the teacher may believe she has found the ideal parents. Will the next few weeks live up to the present euphoria?

Arrange a family council and draw up a timetable which allows for regular, undisturbed practice. Provide opportunities for listening to your child's instrument being played by top-flight professionals, both live and at home, and join those listening periods whenever possible. Ask the teacher to introduce him to other learners. This may in time lead to frequent music making sessions, with or without parental involvement.

Let us assume that you have considered the written or spoken *Conditions for Private Music Instruction*, issued by the teacher. These may, of course, vary from tutor to tutor, but many are switching from the traditional three terms (30 lessons) to four terms per annum (40 lessons). Although these periods do not correspond with school terms, there are still twelve weeks left which can be used to allow time for holiday periods and for making up missed lessons. Apart from more rapid progress resulting from the increased number of lessons, it is not at all fair to expect any teacher to live for 52 weeks on the income of 30. The miracle is that so many have done this for so long.

At the time of writing, the minimum tuition fee suggested by the Incorporated Society of Musicians is around £10 per hour, or pro rata, for private individual lessons. Where two pupils are taught together, each should pay two-thirds the individual tuition fee.

It is occasionally possible to secure lower terms, while quite a few teachers will charge more, but it must not be assumed that the cost of tuition necessarily reflects its quality. Parents should ponder the following points when considering the expense of musical tuition:

1 A plumber's or electrician's call-out fee alone is approximately twice as high as a music teacher's one-hour lesson.

2 The teacher's overheads include maintenance of her studio, lighting and heating; upkeep and repair of her instruments; subscriptions, books, music, stationery; telephone and postage; accounting fees; National Insurance contributions.

3 Tuition fees include preparation for examinations, liaison with parents and schools, aural training and theory instruction, where applicable. In view of all this, an expert teacher's fees are absurdly low, just as an incompetent teacher's fees are too high at any price.

4 The teacher is not entitled to unemployment benefit during the twelve weeks after the fourth term.

Payment for a term's tuition is normally due before the first lesson, and it is perfectly legitimate for a teacher to defer tuition until such payment has been made. Hundreds of teachers have been swindled out of their earnings by defaulters. If you wish to discontinue lessons, written notice should be given by the first lesson of the term, to take effect at its end. The same applies to the teacher who wishes to terminate her tuition. A missed lesson cannot normally be made up, but where the teacher has to cancel a lesson – professional contingencies can make this unavoidable – she will either carry that lesson forward or arrange a refund. As for examinations, concerts and festivals, it should be understood that pupils shall not be entered without the consent of both teachers and parents.

How long should a lesson be? The following Table provides guidelines:

Pupil's Age	Duration of Lesson
5 to 9	half an hour
10 to 13	three quarters of an hour
14 and above	one hour

Quite another way of securing instrumental instruction is via the child's school. Many local education authorities run tuition schemes under which pupils are initially taught in small groups, and later individually. Such instruction is often available on a wide range of instruments, but not always on the piano. This is because schools are anxious to build up their own orchestras, and consequently are looking first of all for string, woodwind and brass players, then for a few percussionists, and possibly for just one keyboard player. Tuition usually begins in the primary school, especially on stringed instruments, since it takes longer for a violinist to reach a respectable standard than, say, a flautist or a trumpeter. Tuition at primary level is often free of charge, while instruments are made available on a loan basis. Nominal sums are sometimes charged towards upkeep and insurance of instruments. Specially talented pupils may graduate from group to individual tuition. When the student commences secondary education, his lessons will continue, but tuition is not necessarily free of charge. As a rule, lessons are no longer in groups, and they take place out of school hours. Pupils are now expected to provide their own instrument, although many authorities run hire schemes. Fees could be expected to be in line with those suggested by the Incorporated Society of Musicians.

When confronted with the choice between private tuition and that provided by the school, parents must consider the advantages and disadvantages. If the tuition takes place at school, parents will have no say in the choice of teacher and not always in the choice of instrument. Although the instructors can be expected to be of good quality, this is not always the case. On the other hand, considerable savings can be made during the first years of tuition. This may help in purchasing a fine instrument later on. Many education authorities guide and supervise their instrumentalists' progress, as illustrated in the following three case histories.

Paula R., aged seven
All children in Paula's infant school were given elementary ear tests, to determine their sense of pitch and general musical awareness. Paula scored well and, in common with five other classmates, she was allocated to the beginners' violin class, permission having been obtained from her parents. A quarter-size violin was made available from the authority-owned pool of instruments, and Paula received her group instruction every Monday during the lunch break. Soon she could manage a few nursery rhymes and simple hymn tunes which she was encouraged to play in class and during school assembly. When she entered junior school, her

tuition continued, but she now shared her lessons with just one other pupil who had made similarly pleasing progress. Her teacher let her take Grade 2 of the Associated Board examinations, and she passed with distinction (141 marks out of 150).

When Paula reached the secondary school stage, she had to leave her teacher and her hired instrument behind, but she was introduced to a new instructor who visited several senior schools in the district after school hours. For her birthday Paula was given a full-size violin by her parents, which her teacher had checked over and recommended. The school ran a flourishing orchestra, but was somewhat short on string players, so Paula was welcomed into the second violin section, where she shared a back desk with a fifth form pupil. Her teacher recommended her to the authority's music adviser, who was in charge of the Saturday Music School, and Paula was invited to attend the String Ensemble which catered for some sixty young players. In her school orchestra she soon advanced to the ranks of the first violins, and at the age of thirteen she was made co-leader. Meanwhile she had passed her Grade 5 examination, this time with a good merit mark (127 out of 150). At fifteen she was promoted from the Saturday String Ensemble to the Symphony Orchestra, moving rapidly from the back of the second to the front of the first violins. She took Music as a GCE 'O' and 'A' level subject and, just before leaving school, she obtained another pass with distinction, in Grade 8 (143 out of 150).

Emma V., aged ten
At her junior school Emma was given the choice of learning the trumpet or the clarinet. Since the family lived in a small flat, they opted for the latter. Had they known about the ear-splitting squeaks a clarinet can produce when encouraged, they would have thought again. However, Emma's clarinet class of four pupils advanced quite rapidly, and before she was twelve she had passed Grade 3 (118 out of 150) and had been presented by an uncle with an instrument of her own.

Unfortunately, the peripatetic clarinet teacher who visited the secondary school was fully booked and had a lengthy waiting list (the clarinet is a most popular instrument), so Emma's parents found her a private teacher. During the next two years, she passed two more examinations, Grade 5 and Grade 6, both with merit (though only just). But, alas, she could not find her way into one of the Saturday Music School orchestras because of the competition for places. She was offered admission to the Music School's Clarinet Choir, but she gave that up after three weeks. 'The caterwauling got on my nerves,' she explained. So she *languished in her school orchestra*, as she put it, never quite recapturing that excitement of her junior school days. Perhaps she should have learned the trumpet after all.

Rustom P., aged fourteen
A late beginner, Rustom took up the French Horn, since that was the only instrument available at his school. His progress, according to his teacher, was 'phenomenal from the first blow'. This is a notoriously problematical instrument to master, being over-responsive to changes of temperature and somewhat unpredictable in its behaviour. Rustom was soon wanted by the school orchestra, and at the same time by the Saturday Combined Schools' Brass Orchestra. At the age of sixteen he had passed Grade 6 with distinction and had become principal horn in the Combined Schools' Symphony Orchestra. He won several first prizes in competitive festivals, then *failed* his Grade 7 examination. His reason? 'My teacher entered me when I was not quite ready, and I went to pieces in the examination room.' His teacher gave quite a different explanation. 'That was the winter when Rustom suffered from severe girlfriend trouble.' However, he retook this grade, passed with a dozen marks to spare, and next year obtained a distinction in Grade 8.

Rustom has travelled with his Saturday Orchestra to West Germany, Denmark and the Netherlands, where they gave several concerts. His performance in Cologne of Mozart's Horn Concerto No. 3 was enthusiastically received. Rustom also took private piano lessons and taught himself composition. He has written some remarkable pieces for chamber ensembles and we shall probably hear more of him.

It can be seen that education authorities who run instrumental tuition schemes offer a wide variety of courses of study and musical experiences. Parents whose children are taught privately should contact their local education offices (see Fact File V) and find out what is on offer, since entry to combined instrumental ensembles is usually not restricted to students who learn under the authority's scheme.

A word of warning to parents. Do not allow yourself to be trapped into providing double tuition for your child. If he learns privately, do not let him have school tuition as well. If he learns at school, do not also engage a private teacher. If you do, your child will almost certainly be forced to cope with conflicting advice and instruction.

Peripatetic teachers are not the only ones who offer tuition in groups. Private teachers, too, have begun to find that group tuition can be stimulating and highly successful when undertaken by teachers who have made a special study of this exciting aspect of instrumental tuition.

FURTHER READING
Bentley: *Musical Ability in Children* (Harrap)
Buck: *Psychology for Musicians* (OUP)
Ching: *Performer and Audience* (Keith Prowse)
Langley: *The Principles of Teaching as Applied to Music* (Hammond)
Lovelock: *Common Sense in Music Teaching* (Bell)
Training Musicians (Gulbenkian Foundation)

POSTSCRIPT
'Those having torches will pass them on to others.'
Plato: *The Republic*

GROUP TUITION
Aural Tests and Theory form part of all graded examinations. Both topics are eminently suitable for group tuition, as has long been recognized by many teachers. But when it comes to instrumental or singing lessons, most teachers prefer individual tuition, in spite of the undeniable success of Piano, Flute and Clarinet tuition in small groups. As for the Violin and the Recorder, it has been demonstrated that pupils in quite large classes can make excellent progress. Although *individual* pupils receive more attention, this must be set against the joy of learning and progressing together with fellow students. Once a pupil has outstripped the others, individual tuition would be indicated.

Any teacher undertaking group tuition should organize her class in such a way that all pupils are involved in the learning process all the time. This requires imagination and a fair degree of resourcefulness. Anyone who has seen Sheila Nelson's London string classes at work will feel enthusiastic about the right sort of group tuition, especially where pupils attend twice a week, once for an individual lesson and once for group coaching.

Teachers and parents might like to consult the following publications:

Enoch: *Group Piano Teaching* (OUP)
Lee: *Group Piano Lessons* (Forsyth)
Nelson: *Moving Up*
Nelson: *Technitunes* } String Tuition (Boosey & Hawkes)
Nelson: *Right From The Start*
Rokos: *String Teaching on a Shoestring* (Bosworth)

The most astonishing development in the field of group tuition is the *Suzuki Method*. Shinichi Suzuki, a Japanese educationist and musician, has repeatedly taken large numbers of his very young pupils on concert tours in the West. Audiences everywhere sit spellbound at the sight of small children playing Bach, Vivaldi and Mozart, in perfect unison and with flawless intonation. While we, the listeners shook our heads in disbelief, a confident smile of pure enjoyment never left the young performers' faces. How is it done?

● 'Talent is not inherited,' says Suzuki, 'and there is no such thing as innate aptitude for music.' To engender a child's musical awareness, he proposes that from the day of his birth (or even while still in his mother's womb) the child should be exposed to music. Suzuki advocates that a short, serene piece of recorded music should be played to the child once every day. There is no need for the music to vary during the next few months.

● Tuition on the Violin begins from the age of three, in small groups, with the mother or father being taught at the same time.

● Parents' involvement is essential. Mother and child or father and child become partners, practising together and learning from each other.

● Since small children enjoy learning through playing, Suzuki teachers show how to play the Violin by playing *with* the Violin (walking while playing; two children sharing one instrument, one bowing, the other fingering, etc etc).

● Instead of teaching the beginner how to stand, how to grip the instrument, how to hold the bow, how to apply it to the strings and how to read music – possibly all at once – the Suzuki method follows a carefully plotted path by taking one step at a time.

● Progress is made by meaningful repetition. The first piece studied is 'Twinkle, twinkle, little star'. The next is 'Twinkle, twinkle, little star', but with slight rhythmic variations, followed by numerous further variations on the same tune.

● As a child learns his mother tongue before he learns to read and write, the Suzuki instrumentalist learns to play by ear, deferring the reading of notation until the end of the first year's tuition.

● After nine months of study, the child's repertoire includes Bach minuets, pieces by Bartók and several nursery rhymes.

Apart from the Violin, the Suzuki Method covers Piano, Cello and Flute. To find out more about it, and to obtain details of Suzuki teachers, contact:

The Administrator, British Suzuki Institute,
The Old School, Brewhouse Hill, Wheathampstead,
Herts AL4 8AN (Tel. 058283 2424)

Parents and teachers may like to consult the following:

Cook: *Suzuki Education In Action* (Exposition Press)
Fryer: *Give Your Child The Right Start* (Souvenir Press)
Suzuki Cello School, with cassettes (Music Sales)
Suzuki: *Nurtured by Love* (Senzay Publications)
Suzuki Piano School, with cassettes (Music Sales)
Suzuki Violin School, with cassettes (Music Sales)

POSTSCRIPT
When a five-year-old girl asked Shinichi Suzuki whether she really had to practise every day, the reply was, 'You don't have to practise on the days you don't eat.'

3 EXAMS AHEAD

Examinations are formidable
even to the best prepared, for
the greatest fool may ask more
than the wisest man can answer.

REV. CHARLES CALEB COLTON

Surveying the field

Sally C., aged fourteen, Violin: 'Too much emphasis is put on what grade you are now and what grade you are going to do next.'

Debbie W., aged twenty-six, Piano: 'Examinations give a pupil something to aim for. They can also take the pleasure out of learning an instrument, if you are pressurized by parents or teacher into taking them.'

These are typical replies to the author's request for information from examinees about their attitude to graded examinations. Most agreed on the desirability of obtaining occasional assessments of their standards of performance. But many were appalled by the monotony which accompanies an unrelenting pursuit of one examination after another. If the gaining of certificates is allowed to determine the nature of a student's tuition, this may well lead to resistance, poor progress and eventual failure. It is interesting to note Regulation 19 of the Trinity College of Music, which states:

A candidate who has passed all practical grade examinations 1–8 in playing a particular instrument is eligible for a Certificate of Special Merit.

Can this be wise?

On the other hand, periodic examinations were liked by most candidates, provided they were well spaced out over a period of time. David V., aged eleven, Flute:

'It gives you something to work for and it gives you a sense of achievement when it's all over.'

Sarah S., aged thirteen, Violin, echoes this:

'I don't like them nor do I dislike them. They are part of playing an instrument. But when I get the exam result I feel a terrific sense of victory.'

This *sense of victory* is, of course, a pleasant sensation, but it will wear off. Far more important is the tonic effect of a passed examination on further effort and further progress.

Rebekah C., aged fourteen, Clarinet:

'I normally go to jelly when I take an exam.'

Poor Rebekah. Could it be that you were not quite ready for that particular grade? Most students find that the extent of their nervousness depends on the thoroughness of their preparation. If the candidate is at least half a grade ahead of the requirements, he will approach the examination with sufficient confidence to control his anxiety. Teachers and parents are well advised to allow for this. But how can one reassure Alex C., aged fourteen, Trumpet, who writes:

'I like *passing* exams, but not *taking* them, because the examiners make you nervous.'

Or Claire T., aged twelve, Violin:

'It depends whether the examiner is good or bad.'

And Natasha C., aged thirteen, Clarinet:

'I do not like to perform in front of total strangers.'

The vast majority of examiners belong to the human race. They possess musical expertise and they are experienced in dealing sympathetically with children and adults. Their first concern is to put the candidates at their ease. Some do this by chatting briefly about football or TV, others through a friendly smile. Rare indeed, and almost extinct, is the ogre who sits at his desk and, without looking up, bellows 'Name?', scribbles, growls 'Grade?', scribbles, spits 'Piece?', scribbles, and grunts 'Begin!' The author once encountered him, but that is so long ago that he is likely to have shut up shop. Maybe he just petrifies the night nurse these days.

James P., aged fifteen, Viola, reports:

'I think music exams are a good idea, though some of the pieces you have to play are rather dull.'

James has a point. Although the lists from which the music is chosen contain a good deal of worthwhile matter, some pieces are less interesting than the rest. It is up to the teacher to spot the music which will keep her pupils' interest alive over a period of months. Inevitably, some pieces are technically slightly less demanding, but if they lack appeal they should be

115

avoided. An *easy* piece, played correctly but listlessly, will gain fewer marks than a *hard* one, played with musical conviction.

A crucial point is raised by Aron G., aged fourteen, Violin:

'I think the examiner should be able to play the instrument that is being examined.'

This seems a most reasonable request. As a violinist, Aron feels that an examiner who is also a string player may well be more appreciative of those technical aspects in his performance which a non-specialist might miss. Quite so. Examiners, however, tend to examine everything, including those instruments they play themselves and those they do not. Why? Let us return to Aron. If his examiner had been an expert on the Violin, he would not only comment on deficiencies in Aron's playing, if any, but in his desire to be helpful he might suggest measures to be taken to remedy such shortcomings. Since there are many methods of teaching an instrument, or the voice, it is quite feasible that the teacher's methods differ from the examiner's. The latter's report on Aron's performance could, therefore, provoke more problems than it solves. This author, when examining, would always endeavour to judge a performance by its effect on the listener. If it fulfils the composer's demands, he would be satisfied. In other words, the result is of greater significance than the means by which it is achieved, and a trumpeter can give a considered verdict on a harpist's performance, as long as he is an accomplished musician. Or, on a slightly flippant level, to appreciate a good egg you need not be able to lay one.

Finally, here is a noteworthy point, raised by Jacqueline G., aged fifteen, Saxophone:

'Exams are helpful, but they are expensive.'

Added to the cost of an instrument, of tuition, of accessories and of printed music, examination fees certainly constitute an extra expense. The more reason for not entering them rashly. This Table sets out the current costs.

Grade	AB	G Brass	Perc.	others	T	L
1	9.50	9.00	14.30	8.00	7.90	7.80
2	11.50	9.75	14.30	9.35	7.90	8.40
3	11.50	11.00	14.30	9.60	10.40	9.40
4	13.50	11.60	16.20	11.00	11.70	10.50
5	13.50	14.00	18.30	11.55	13.00	11.50
6	15.00	16.00	19.50	12.50	14.50	12.60
7	17.00	19.50	20.00	14.00	16.00	14.20
8	20.00	21.50	21.50	17.00	18.80	16.20

In a previous chapter the futility of *shopping around* for the 'best' examination syllabus has been discussed. So how is one to decide? Obtain Regulations and Syllabuses from all four boards. First, find out whether your subject is covered. If you will turn back to pp. xi–xii, you will see that only Associated Board and Trinity offer an examination in Harpsichord playing, while Guildhall omits the Double Bass and London the Tuba, and neither London nor Associated Board cater for Percussion. Next, ascertain whether there is an examination centre in your vicinity. Then decide which syllabus appeals to you, not forgetting such details as examination dates in various parts of the country. It is not within the province of this book to discuss the relative standing of the various examination boards, but the number of their examiners suggests their volume of business. At the time of writing, Associated Board calls upon 517 examiners, Guildhall 86, Trinity 70 and London 96.

The four boards do not show significant variations in their examination requirements. All offer a choice of pieces to be performed, and all include Scales and Arpeggios, Aural Tests, Sight Reading and questions on Rudiments of Music. Guildhall, Trinity and London allocate marks for their Viva Voce or General Musicianship sections, while Associated Board (until 1989) incorporates such marks in their allocation for the Sight Reading test. This results in a disparity between the four examining bodies in respect of percentage marks awarded to the various parts of the examination. The following four examples illustrate this point:

	AB Piano Grade 3	G Flute Grade 2	T Violin Grade 5	L Clarinet Grade 7
Pieces and Studies	60%	57%	60%	60%
Scales and Arpeggios	14%	15%	15%	15%
Aural Tests	12%	10%	10%	8%
Sight Reading	14%	9%	10%	10%
Viva Voce/Gen. Mus.	–	9%	5%	7%

Pieces and studies

The wise teacher agrees with her pupils on a judicious choice of pieces. She will try to match the music on offer with her pupils' taste. She will advocate pieces that present a challenge both technically and musically, and she will introduce the music to her students by playing it to them. She will also locate any existing recordings of such works. It is advisable, however, to discriminate between performances of examination music recorded by anonymous players which may fall short of artistic merit, and recordings by artists whose playing can inspire and help to improve the listener's performance.

A welcome recording service for instrumentalists and singers exists in the *Music Minus One** series of recordings. Although their catalogue caters for more advanced players, it offers the invaluable experience of joining up with an accompanist, a group or a whole orchestra whose sounds – minus your own – are recorded on tape or on discs. Thus, a pianist can play Debussy's duet, *Petite Suite*, with another pianist, or the Piano part of a Beethoven Trio with a violinist and cellist. He can even be the star performer in Beethoven's *Emperor Concerto*, which has been recorded minus the solo Piano. Likewise, a Viola player can join a string quartet, a flautist can meet an accompanist, the trumpeter a brass ensemble, the singer can team up with a pianist, and a jazz clarinettist with a Big Band.

As for the Study which is often required as the third piece to be performed, the teacher should impress its dual purpose on her pupils: the technical progress which results from study and mastery, and the opportunity of charming the examiner with a faultless performance which, if it is played with musical sensitivity, will boost the marks total. The pieces should present a contrast. Avoid two slow and sad ones, or two fast and jolly ones. Well before the examination date the candidate ought to be able to play his prepared music with some degree of confidence and ease, so that he can concentrate on its *musical* content, convincing the examiner that he has found and is able to convey the mood and the meaning of each of his pieces. This can be achieved, provided the examination requirements fall slightly short of the student's standard at the time of the examination. It is a self-defeating exercise to allow a student to struggle against a deadline. In an ideal world no student need ever fail an examination.

In recent years a whole industry has sprung up which provides candidates with study aids in the shape of specially recorded music of examination pieces, most of them catering for Grades 1 to 7. If used wisely, they can be helpful, although they do not replace a good teacher. The danger lies in imitating the style of performance, thus stifling one's own initiative and musical convictions. Associated Board have gone so far as to print a prominently displayed note in their syllabus which warns against the 'growing number of commercial cassette recordings of its examination music, some of which have imperfections in both performance and quality of reproduction', and it advises teachers and candidates

* Forsyth, 126 Deansgate, Manchester 3.

'not to regard them as definitive interpretations . . . but to use their own discretion in achieving a musical performance.' Guildhall, on the other hand, undaunted and enterprisingly issues its own *Cassettes of Examination Pieces and Aural Tests* for all Grades up to Grade 6. These are obtainable from their Publications Department.

You may care to try one or more of the following products, some of which are excellent both in performance and technical quality:

Ass. Bd. Examination Music (Piano and Violin), Grades 1–7.
Sound Wise, 23 Frithville Gdns, London W12 7JG

Bruche Ass. Bd. Examination Pieces (Piano, Violin, Woodwind), Grades 1–7, 1–5 and 3–6 resp.
International Music Services, 47–53 St John St, London EC1

Kenneth van Barthold's Piano Examination Pieces, Grade 1–7.
Sound News Studios, 18 Blenheim Rd, London W4 1ES

Piano Pieces for Ass. Bd. Examinations, Grades 1–7.
Hattrick Music Services, 33 Goodmayes Lane, Ilford, Essex IG3 9PB

Scales and arpeggios

It makes little sense for a teacher to confront her pupils with a pack of scales and arpeggios, informing them that these are the requirements for their particular grade, and they had better practise them. Where is the motivation? Young students cannot be expected to realize, but have every right to know, that practically every piece of music contains scale and arpeggio passages, and that the purpose and indeed the beauty of growing up on a diet of scales and arpeggios lies in its prolific effect on further effort. The teacher should point out such passages in music by various composers and demonstrate how a great deal of repetitive work can be cut short by scrupulous attention to this section of the syllabus. She might mention that there are only a few scales to be learnt, but once perfected they need hardly be practised again when encountered in *real music*. The obvious analogy with athletics may convince the doubters, since a *generally* fit person is also fit for *specific* activities, be it cricket, volleyball, athletics or the ability to concentrate on a book after hours of tiring homework.

Scales and arpeggios (or, in early grades, broken chords) should be even and fluent. There should be little hesitation in responding to the examiner's requests, and in the higher grades the speed should be enterprising but not hazardous.

In the author's experience, quite a few candidates fail to do themselves justice by being obviously unprepared in this department. He has met teachers who blithely announced that practising scales was not worth the effort 'for a mere 15 marks'. He has also met far too many candidates who were patently unfamiliar with elementary musical terminology. Examiner: 'Please play a scale in E melodic minor.' Candidate: 'What is melodic, sir?'

Teachers of younger children may find a useful ally in *Supascales* with its Scale Box which, according to its publishers, 'not only makes the business of practising scales more attractive to young children, but it also saves the instrumental teacher valuable time.'*

Aural tests

It is strange that the key to musical appreciation and its performance, the key that opens the door to *all* music, has been landed with the cheerless name tag *Aural Training*.

The person with a poor aural sense will not only gain low marks in that particular examination section, but his enjoyment of music will be severely curtailed. Not for him the thrill of spotting a counter-melody played by an Oboe, when all the untrained ear can pick out is the main tune played by Trumpets and Violins. Not for him the fascination of becoming immersed in a Haydn Piano Trio or a Beethoven String Quartet, where the trained ear follows each instrument, obtaining a sound picture as the composer designed it. The person with poor listening powers lives with a massive handicap, the equivalent to the colour blind in a picture gallery.

Aural Tests devised by the four major examination bodies investigate a candidate's sense of time, pitch and rhythm, musical memory, powers of concentration and speed of reaction. As an example, the following Table lists the requirements for Grade 1.

AB	G	T	L
The examiner plays a note between middle C and treble C. Sing it.	The examiner plays two notes chosen from the key note, 2nd, 3rd, 5th or upper octave of a major scale, twice. Sing them.	The examiner plays C, followed by either C, D, E, F or G. Sing both notes and describe the interval.	The examiner plays the common chord of C major, followed by one of its notes. Identify it.

* *Supascales*: Dennetts, Broughton, Stockbridge, Hants SO20 8AD.

AB	G	T	L
The examiner plays a major key chord followed by the key note, followed by either the 2nd, 3rd, 4th or 5th note. Say which.	The examiner plays the key chord of C or G major (he will say which), followed by the key note, followed by either the 2nd, 3rd, 5th or upper octave. Describe the interval.		The examiner plays a short unfinished melody. Sing its key note.
	The examiner plays 3 notes between middle C and the C above, twice. Say which is the highest *or* the lowest note.	The examiner plays a simple harmonic phrase, twice. Say whether it is major or minor.	The examiner plays 3 notes in a major key. Sing them.
The examiner plays a short melody, twice. Clap its rhythm.	The examiner plays a short melody, twice. Clap its rhythm.	The examiner plays a short melody, twice. Clap its rhythm.	The examiner plays a simple melody in 2/4 time (probably twice, though the syllabus does not say so). Clap its rhythm.
The examiner plays some music in either 2 or 3 time. When he plays it again, beat time to it.	The examiner repeats the same passage. When he plays it once more, beat time to it.		The examiner plays a melody, mostly in crotchets. Beat time.

Consult the syllabuses for detailed requirements of all other grades. Specimen Aural Tests can be obtained:

AB Specimen Aural Tests Grades 1 to 5, Grades 6 to 7, Grade 8. 90p each.

G Specimen Aural Tests for each Grade, published separately. 20p each.

T Sample Ear Tests for Grade Examinations (all Grades). £1.40.

L Specimen Ear Tests (all Grades). £1.50.

Armed with these resources, the instrumental or singing teacher can proceed with aural instruction, by setting aside a brief part of each lesson for this purpose. Yet many candidates fail to score well in this area. With the various examination bodies awarding between 8 and 12 per cent maximum marks for Aural Tests, a poor result in this part of the examination can make the difference between a good or a mere pass, or between pass and failure. Why, then, are Aural Tests a bed of thorns for so many candidates? Here are the reasons.

1 No clear understanding has been reached between parents and teachers, prior to commencement of lessons. If a teacher agrees to prepare her pupil for an examination, it does not necessarily follow that she will cover aural training in addition to her instrumental or vocal tuition.

2 While most teachers are scrupulous in studying the examination syllabus, there are some whose inexperience prevents them from designing a course of instruction which covers *all* requirements.

3 Since the prepared pieces can gain a maximum of between 54 and 60 per cent of the total marks, it is often assumed that studying those pieces should precede both aural training and scales and arpeggios. Such a cart-before-horse procedure overlooks the guiding influence of scales and arpeggios on the technical proficiency of a candidate's examination music, and of aural training on its musical quality. The wise teacher is aware of the universality of music. Therefore all her lessons will incorporate all aspects of the syllabus.

4 Where a teacher is fortunate in dealing with a specially gifted pupil, she may be tempted to ignore aural training, trusting that the student's innate musicality will pull him through. It hardly ever does.

5 Perhaps the most common blunder is to regard Aural Tests as a necessary evil and the process of aural training as a chore. This error arises from a misunderstanding of the test requirements. For example, AB Grade 5 Aural Test asks you 'to sing the upper or lower note of an interval played harmonically and to describe it as a major 2nd, major 3rd,

perfect 4th, perfect 5th, major 6th, major 7th or an octave'. Admittedly, this sounds a bit gloomy, but in fact it is entirely practical. Let us particularize. The examiner plays an interval on the Piano, say middle C and the G above, asking you to sing the lower note. If you can do this, you will probably be able to sing the lower part in a choir – a joyful skill – and to follow an inner melodic line when listening to an orchestra. The examiner then asks you to define the interval. If you answer correctly, *perfect 5th*, you will have demonstrated, among other things, your ability to tune your own Violin or Cello. It should always be remembered that the examination requirements are not an end in itself, but a reflection of a successful course of aural training.

Ideally, however, aural training ought to begin long before the student's first lesson with his teacher, and the place for it is *home*. As soon as the young child shows signs of musical curiosity, aural training should commence. Or should we say aural retraining? A tiny baby's hearing is acute. It swiftly learns to discriminate between welcome and unwelcome sounds, between meaningful and irrelevant ones, such as mother's voice and its association with comfort and food, and her receding footsteps and its association with tedium; the pleasurable twittering of birds, and the inconsequential patter of rain. As the baby grows into an infant, he acquires amongst his numerous new skills the ability to exclude or minimize unwelcome sounds, much as adults do when they wish to engage in conversation against some *musical* background in a restaurant or hotel lobby. Over a period of time, this automatic aural self-defence can lead to some blunting of aural perception which needs the antidote of aural retraining. The proposed method, as will be shown, is entirely pleasurable, and its objective is no less than the acquisition of a passport to the world of music, a target which accommodates but goes beyond the passing of aural examinations.

Parents who are prepared to participate in the course of aural training in the guise of musical games, as described below, need no specific knowledge, but they will gain, together with their children, an understanding of the rudiments of music and an acute aural awareness which is a precondition for the enjoyment of music.

Rhythm

A Mrs Watson claps her name, Mary Watson = ♩ ♩ ♩ ♩ . Each note stands for a syllable, and each underline signifies a strong beat. To demonstrate the difference between strong and weak beats, clap the strong and tap the weak ones. Mr Watson claps and taps his name, Derek Watson = ♩ ♩ ♩ ♩ . Their son does likewise. Peter Watson

123

= ♩ ♪ ♩ ♪. Daughter Veronica has a harder task. Veronica Watson
= ♩ ♩ ♩ ♩ ♩ ♩. Vary this game by clapping and tapping the names of
other relatives, friends and famous or infamous people. Clap and tap a
name for the others to guess. For example, say, 'I am a northern
suburb of London', clap and tap ♩ ♩ ♩ ♩ ♩ ♩. The correct answer is
Welwyn Garden City. Later – sometimes much later – write the names
down, first in simplified notation as above, then inserting bar lines
before each strong beat, and omitting the underlines, thus:

Mary Watson = | ♩ ♩ | ♩ ♩ .

Veronica Watson = ♩ | ♩ ♩ ♩ | ♩ ♩ .

Once the principle of strong and weak beats and of different
rhythm patterns has been established in everybody's mind, proceed to
drawing attention to the difference between 2 and 3 beats in a bar,
and amend the previous notation to:

Mary Watson = $\frac{2}{4}$ ♩ ♩ | ♩ ♩ .

Veronica Watson = $\frac{3}{4}$ ♩ | ♩ ♩ ♩ | ♩ ♩.

Explain that $\frac{2}{4}$ and $\frac{3}{4}$ are *time signatures*, that the lower figure 4 is a kind
of shorthand for *beats* or *beats in a bar*, without going into further
details at this stage, and that the time signature replaces the initial
bar line. Clap and tap names of towns and countries. 'What country
am I?': $\frac{3}{4}$ ♩ ♩ ♩. (Answer: *Germany* or *Italy* or *Portugal* etc.) It is a
short step from here to introducing 4 beats in a bar, as in *Peterborough
Advertiser* = $\frac{4}{4}$ ♩ ♩ ♩ ♩ | ♩ ♩ ♩ ♩.

B Procure a tape or record of some uncomplicated music (or play the
Piano, if you can), such as waltzes and marches. Everybody claps the
strong beats. Then ask one member of the group to clap the strong
beats, and another to tap the weak beats. At a given sign let them
change over, from strong to weak, and from weak to strong. This is
not easy, but it teaches mind and body to respond to rhythmical
effects. This in turn leads to a more meaningful understanding of the
rudiments of music, and what we are pleased to call the *Theory of
Music* becomes the *Practice of Music.*

C Clap a rhythm, any rhythm. Ask the others to repeat it after you.
You may have to give them two or three chances. Start with short,
easy patterns. Proceed to longer, more complicated ones.

D Clap a well known tune, twice or three times. Ask the others to
identify it. Then let members of the group clap their own tunes and
request identification.

E Any number can play. For instance mother, father, child, child, friend. Mother claps and taps steady beats, 4 in a bar, not too fast. Father nods his head on each first beat. Child One raises his eyebrows on each second beat. Child Two turns full circle on each third beat. Friend opens and shuts his mouth on each fourth beat. Vary responses and number of participants ad infinitum.

Dynamics

A Sit in a circle. One group member is blindfolded. The others recite the alphabet, slowly, with different dynamics, e.g. one speaks pianissimo, another piano, another forte, another fortissimo. The blindfolded member is to spot the quietest and the loudest. Change over, until everybody has had a turn.

B Same procedure as before, but instead of speaking the letters of the alphabet, all sing the same song with different dynamics.

C Same procedure again, but this time all clap steady beats, dynamics ranging from pp to ff.

D This is best played outdoors. One group member is blindfolded. Place human obstacles along a winding course which the blindfolded has to negotiate. Number your obstacles from 1 to 4 or more, and ask them to whisper their respective numbers, to guide the blindfolded along the obstacle course.

Played with sufficient variations, these games cannot fail to improve your aural perception dramatically. But the king of all aural games is the *Matchbox*. Get hold of a box of matches, not the super size nor the flat variety, but the ordinary household kind. This game is best played by two partners. You will find approximately forty matches inside the box. Take them all out. Now hold the empty box close to your right or left ear and shake it (the box!). Since there is no rattling sound, you are right in assuming the box is empty. No, that is not the game yet. Place one single match inside the box, rattle it close to either ear and familiarize yourself with the resultant sound. Now add nine further matches, making a total of ten. Rattle the box and listen. Can you tell the difference between one and ten matches? Test your partner and let your partner test you. At this stage the box contains either one or ten matches. The next step is a full box of approximately forty matches. Again, test your partner and let your

125

partner test you. If you procure several boxes each, you can prepare them beforehand, with your own secret code marking boxes containing one, ten or forty matches. After some time you should experiment with two further and rather more difficult tasks: boxes containing five and twenty matches respectively. Once you can differentiate between one and ten matches, you might – with practice – respond correctly to the five matches, whose rattle is quieter than ten, but louder than one. Similarly, half the box – twenty – will be louder than ten but quieter than the full box of forty. You will find that fives and twenties are far harder than the rest, but not impossible.

Rattle each box twice, once for each ear. Score as follows:

Matches	Score
1	2
5	5
10	3
20	5
40	3

When you begin to score top marks consistently, your ears are as sharp as they ever will be, as sharp in fact as they were when you were a baby.

Recognition of instruments

Being able to name the instruments of the orchestra, not only by their appearance but by their sound, is an achievement worth striving for. It adds a new dimension to your powers of listening which, in turn, enhances your appreciation of music, while taking your aural training another stage further. Invest in a recording of the instruments of the orchestra, such as the one introduced by Yehudi Menuhin. This is now available on cassette tape (John Hosier: *Instruments of the Orchestra*, OUP), with an informative accompanying booklet which includes clear pictures of all instruments. Yehudi Menuhin describes each instrument, before its range, tone quality and technical features are demonstrated by professional players.

All orchestral instruments are covered, from Violin to Cymbals, and you can hear them first as solo instruments, and then in their orchestral environment. For instance, the Violin demonstrates its open strings, its full range, its way of coping with changing dynamics by playing a section of a *Chaconne* by Bach, followed by various methods of bowing (*saltellato, martellato, tremolo* and *col legno*). *Double stopping* can be heard in 'Drink to me only', use of the *mute* in an extract from Mozart's Concerto in G major, *harmonics* are explained, and after a *pizzicato* passage the section ends with the Violins of the Berlin Philharmonic in full flight, in the finale of Brahms' Symphony No. 1. In the woodwind group, for a further example, we hear the Clarinet (played by Jack Brymer) displaying its range and tone quality, first by itself, then in brief extracts from Tchaikovsky's Symphony No. 5 and Mendelssohn's *Fingal's Cave*. This is followed by a comparison of Clarinet and Flute in a passage from Tchaikovsky's *Sleeping Beauty*, while two Clarinets playing in different registers can be heard in the Trio section of Mozart's Symphony No. 39. Similarly, all the other orchestral instruments are put through their paces, including the Percussion section, which presents three Kettle-drums, a *pedal glissando*, an extract from the *Symphonie Fantastique* by Berlioz, a roll and single strokes on the Bass Drum and Side Drum, Cymbal clashes, a roll from *ppp* to *fff*, and edges of Cymbals brushed against each other.

In short, here is musical treasure. Live for a while with the tape and its booklet, learn more and more about the instruments, lodge their sounds in your memory, and emerge as a well informed connoisseur with a newly gained power of discriminating listening.

Much pleasure and further insight may be gained from listening to Benjamin Britten's *Young Person's Guide to the Orchestra*. This is really a set of orchestral variations on a theme by Henry Purcell, in the course of which Britten displays first the sections of the orchestra, and then each instrument in turn. It all ends with a fugue in which the instruments appear once more, one after another, until strings, woodwind and percussion join in Britten's fugue theme, while the brass play the original theme by Purcell.

Pitch

Game A An adult member of the group sings or plays a rising melodic line. The listeners rise from a seated position, following the rising melody. When it falls, they drop with it, and likewise respond physically to all further ascents, descents, twists and turns. Young children do not always understand adult terminology, such as *high* and *low* in music, causing their bewildered elders to exclaim, 'Can't you hear this is a high note and this is a low note?' The child can hear very well that the notes differ in pitch, but he needs to be told that a bird twitters *high* and a lion growls *low*. Once this is established, you can play the game.

B An adult sings or plays a snatch of a tune. The listeners echo this as

127

accurately as possible. Initially the adult can sing or play the phrase three times before the echo answers. With growing confidence this can be reduced to twice and eventually to once only. The game can be developed into a combined pitch-and-dynamics game. Place two or more children in various parts of the room and request a crescendo or decrescendo echo, like this:

Adult – sings or plays phrase *mf* (medium loud)
First child – echoes *pp*
Second Child – echoes *p*
Third child – imitates *f*, and vice versa.

C Four play the *Organ Game*. Three children hold out their right hands, palms upwards, and respond to the player by singing predetermined notes as the player touches their hands. For example:

First Child – responds by singing Doh (first note of scale)
Second Child – responds by singing Me (third note of scale)
Third Child – responds by singing Soh (fifth note of scale).

This way the organ player can elicit the beginning of *The Blue Danube*, thus:

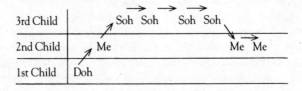

This and similar patterns can later lead to elementary notation, thus:

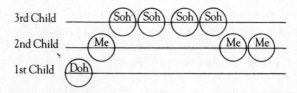

D Listen to some fairly slow music on your radio/tape recorder/ record player. Turn the treble control to its extreme position, let the others listen, then switch it right down while boosting the bass control. Again let everybody listen, until they are fairly sure that they can tell the difference. Turn the whole thing into a game by awarding points for correct responses.

E A much neglected but immensely effective aid for pitch control are the Tonic Sol-fa handsigns. Most children learn at school to sing the scale on the traditional names:

1st note of scale	Doh	5th note of scale	Soh
2nd note of scale	Ray	6th note of scale	Lah
3rd note of scale	Me	7th note of scale	Te
4th note of scale	Fah	8th note of scale	Doh

But few teachers employ the accompanying handsigns which were introduced in the nineteenth century by the great musical educator John Curwen. All members of the group can learn his signs quite rapidly. This is what they look like:

Doh   Ray   Me   Fah   Soh   Lah   Te

The three notes forming the common chord, Doh – Me – Soh (or C – E – G, in C major), are the fundamental ones. Hence the fist for Doh, the vertically outstretched hand with the upwards pointing thumb for Soh, and in between the horizontal hand for Me. Between Doh and Me rises the diagonally pointing Ray, while between Me and Soh the downward-pointing Fah indicates its tendency for sinking down to Me, the note below. Another such strange liking of one note for a neighbouring one exists in Te, the 7th note of the scale, which often wishes to rise to the 8th note, the octave Doh. The handsign for Te, therefore, is the finger pointing upwards towards Doh. Finally, Lah or the 6th note of the scale, hangs bell-like above Soh, the 5th note.

When you have learnt the handsigns, sing a scale (it need not be C major), while showing each note with your hands, one at first, both later on. If one of you can play that scale at the same time on the Piano, Recorder or any other instrument, all the better. Now experiment:

1   Sing and display Doh – Soh, the interval of a fifth. Get used to its sound.

Add Lah, to experience the suspended-bell quality of that 6th note of the scale, as it hangs above Soh. Sing and display Doh – Soh – Lah – Soh.

Sing and display the same notes, but this time each one twice, then go right down the scale:

Doh – Doh – Soh – Soh – La – La – Soh

Fah – Fah – Me – Me – Ray – Ray – Doh.
You have sung and displayed 'Twinkle, twinkle, little star'. Splendid.

We investigate the love relationship between Fah and Me, and between Te and Doh. Sing and display an ascending scale. One of you stops at Fah and hangs on to it, while the others continue to Te and hold that note. Take a breath when needed and continue sounding Fah, the 4th note of the scale, against Te, the 7th. Can you feel how the Fah wants to fall to Me, and how the Te yearns for its Doh? Fulfil their desire:

$$\left(\begin{array}{l} Te \longrightarrow Doh \\ Fah \longrightarrow Me \end{array} \right)$$

2 Repeat this several times, changing parts. You have established an important law in music. The interval Fah-Te is a discord (an augmented fourth, if you want to know), but the interval Me-Doh (octave above) is a concord (a minor sixth). The law says, *A discord has an inbuilt tendency to resolve itself into a concord.* If you consult your dictionary, you will find:

Discord: lack of harmony, disagreement, dissonance.
Concord: agreement, peaceful relationship.
Perhaps there is a lesson here for us all.

3 One person displays handsigns, the others sing:

Baa baa, black sheep, have you   a–ny   wool?
Doh Doh Soh Soh   Lah Te Doh Lah Soh

Yes sir, yes sir, three bags full.
Fah Fah Me Me Ray Ray Doh

One for the master   and one for the dame,
Soh Soh Soh Fah Fah   Fah Me Me Me Ray

and one for the little   boy who lives down the lane.
Ray Soh Soh Soh Fah Soh La Fah Me Ray Ray Doh.

Further examples:

'Lavender's blue' (begins on Doh)
'Frère Jacques' (begins on Doh)
'The first Nowell' (begins on Me)
'Drink to me only' (begins on Me).

130

Growlers

Scene: Classroom, Chopin Comprehensive, Ennitown.
Time: Now.
Characters: Choirmaster, boys and girls.

Thirty more or less silvery voices attempt to do justice to 'Greensleeves'. Or rather twenty-nine, for somewhere there is a drone which refuses to budge from its monotone. And now the teacher has spotted him. 'Stop that horrible noise, boy. Sit over there, on the growlers' bench.' The unsuspecting offender had not really been aware of his crime, but now he knew. He was a growler. Nature had made him a growler. He would probably always be a growler.

What can be done about this? Must we exclude an inept minority from the pleasurable pursuits of an adroit majority? Is there such a thing as tone-deafness?

A good deal of research has led many experts to believe that only a tiny percentage of children exhibit signs of genuine tone-deafness which can often be traced to a physical or mental handicap. The overwhelming number of growlers suffer from some form of inhibition which makes them prefer the *safety* of the monotone to the hazard of venturing into lower and higher regions. Many growlers enjoy their *singing*, until they are told not to. This reinforces their inhibition, and they are likely to abstain from pleasures which were not meant for them.

There is a cure for hypothetical tone-deafness, and teachers and parents can perform it, provided they muster enough patience, optimism and good humour. Let the growler take part in all pitch games which were outlined above, without taking much note of faulty responses. Set aside short, regular individual sessions, where you locate his monotone pitch (growlers are of either gender, but for brevity's sake we shall use the masculine pronoun). Let us assume his *home* note is F above middle C. Play his note on any available instrument, or sing it with him. Now encourage him to venture a little higher. Play or sing for him:

F   F   F G F   F   C
Good King Wenceslas looked out

Ask him to join in. It does not matter at this stage whether he pitched the G correctly, as long as he rose anywhere above F. It is quite possible that he will descend to the vicinity of the lower C before he will rise to the higher G. You will have to repeat this process many times, but one day

131

the breakthrough will be achieved, when he moves away from the shelter of his monotone. When it happens, be lavish with your praise. Introduce frequent diversions during those training sessions. Ask him to sing or shout or whisper his highest note. Then his lowest note. Anything, to tempt him up and down. Let him imitate a siren, rising and falling. Create opportunities for him to take part in some unsophisticated community singing, perhaps at the level of a non-Welsh football chorus. Once he has ventured from monotone to notes in the immediate neighbourhood, you will find it takes less time to entice him further afield, until you can pronounce him an ex-growler. You have taught a supposedly lame person to walk again.

Games involving rhythm, dynamics and pitch, and purposeful listening to the instruments of the orchestra have prepared the ground for the instrumental or singing teacher to begin her course of specialized aural training which leads to – and should lead beyond – the examination requirements. What has been an aural adventure now becomes an aural discipline. Without the former, it would be arduous work indeed for the latter. Employing an analogy from the field of sport, we have concentrated on achieving a respectable degree of fitness, before specializing in pole vaulting or figure skating. A well trained ear should find it both uncomplicated and pleasurable to cope with such examination questions as:

> Clap the rhythm-pattern of a short melody played twice. (AB, Grade 2)

This has been covered in Rhythm Game C. Or:

> Hum or sing a four-bar melody after hearing it twice. (T, Grade 4)

Anyone who has played Pitch Game B will sail through this. Or:

> Sing any degree of a major or harmonic minor scale above a given key note, after having heard the key note sounded and the required degree named. (G, Grade 6)

Pitch Game E and its hand signs has taken you almost there. As a further memory aid, you may care to remember the various intervals by some well known music, like this:

Interval	Memory aid
Major Second	<u>She'll be</u> coming round the mountain
Minor Third	Greensleeves: <u>Alas,</u> my love
Major Third	Blue Danube, first two notes
Perfect Fourth	Auld Lang Syne: <u>Should auld</u> acquaintance be forgot
Perfect Fifth	<u>All Glo</u>ry, laud and honour
Minor Sixth	<u>When Is</u>rael was in Egypt's land
Major Sixth	<u>My bonn</u>ie lies over the ocean
Major Seventh	<u>Some</u>where <u>o</u>ver the rainbow
Octave	<u>Somewhere</u> over the rainbow

Or the question may be:

Hum or sing the middle or lowest note of a major or minor triad. (L, Grade 8)

Listening to the whole range of orchestral instruments, and following them in their natural habitat, has enabled you to pick out notes other than top notes. You will find this easy.

Further aural requirements, such as recognizing cadences and distinguishing between major, minor and diminished triads, can now be tackled with confidence. Many teachers have in recent years established a practice of holding aural training sessions in groups, usually on the weekends. This is to be applauded, especially since such group activities form a natural extension to the earlier aural games.

A bewildering array of publications, teaching aids and cassette tapes are on offer, for the use of teachers and their pupils. The following are recommended:

Allchin: *Aural Training* (Novello)
Hindemith: *Aural Training* (Schott)
Jersild: *Ear Training* (Chester)
Self: *Aural Adventure* (Novello)
Taylor: *A Method of Aural Training* (OUP)

Cassette tapes, covering various examination syllabuses, can be obtained from these sources:

Aural Training Cassettes, Ass. Board, all Grades.
C. Lees, 9 Shear Bank Gdns, Blackburn, BB1 8AY.

133

Bruche Associated Board Aural Tests, all Grades.
  Chester Music, 7–9 Eagle Court, London EC1M 5QD.
Guildhall School of Music and Drama Cassettes of Aural Tests for all
  instruments, all Grades.
  GSMD, Publications Dept, Barbican, London EC2Y 8DT.
How to do Aural Tests for Ass. Board examinations, all grades. Also:
Recognition of Cadences and Chords.
  Hattrick Music Services, 33 Goodmayes Lane,
  Ilford, Essex IG3 9PB.
Self-Help Aural Tests for Examinations in Music.
  M. Illman, 47 Barton Rd, Woodbridge, Suffolk IP12 1JH.
Sound Sense Aural Test Cassettes, all Grades.
  Sound News Studios, 18 Blenheim Rd, London W4 1ES.
Sound Wise Ass. Board Aural Test Cassettes, all Grades.
  Sound Wise, 23 Frithville Gdns, London W12 7JG.

An excellent, non-specific publication is:

W. Salaman: *Listening In*, 3 vols plus 3 Teacher's Books and Cassette.
  Middle Eight Music, 23 Garrick St, London WC2 9AX.

Mention should be made here of Joseph Cooper's intriguing *Hidden Melodies* and its sequel, *More Hidden Melodies* (Paxton). Devotees of BBC Television's *Face the Music* will remember those ingenious piano pieces, played by Cooper in the style of a famous composer, which contain a popular tune, deftly hidden somewhere in the texture of the music. For example, 'Three blind mice' in the style of Bach, 'For he's a jolly good fellow' in the style of Chopin, or 'The Londonderry Air' in the style of Brahms. Get a competent pianist to play these for you and have hours of musical fun. Truly, Aural Training without tears.

Sight reading

One of the intimate joys of playing an instrument and/or singing is the constant opportunity for *browsing*. The pianist, the flautist, the violinist, the singer, the trumpeter can daily add to their knowledge of the repertoire, simply by dipping into a page here, a few bars there. Accuracy of notes is less important here than obtaining glimpses of the kind of music one tackles. As your familiarity with the repertoire grows, your skill in coping with the music will increase, with a corresponding decrease in the number of note errors. Start with music that looks easier than the music you are studying. Do not hesitate to leave out any number of notes, as long as you keep the music moving along, not at a gallop, but at a steady trot. Your guide lines are:

1 Keep strict time, however slowly.
2 Go for rhythmical accuracy, even at the expense of note accuracy.
3 Never, never stop to repeat anything at all.

Once you have formed the habit of regular browsing, you are bound to grow in confidence and expertise. You will be able to omit fewer notes, because you recognize familiar patterns. The keyboard player will shed his fear of thick clusters of chords, because he has taught himself to look at the top and the bottom notes, while his fingers fill in the harmony suggested by those notes. This does not always work, but often it will. Anyway, the more periods you spend at this hobby, the greater the number of notes you will be able to take in at first sight. Your motto: *Boldness be my friend.*

The Associated Board awards a maximum of 14 per cent for Sight Reading, a whole 5 per cent more than Guildhall, and 4 per cent more than Trinity and London. Daily attention to that section of your musical endeavour will therefore not only turn you into a more versatile musician, but you will gather valuable marks which might take you from pass to merit, or from merit to the top.

Wind instrument candidates entered for an Associated Board examination and their teachers should note that in Grades 1 to 4 the Sight Reading tests start with a short Viva Voce session. (This applies, however, only until 1989.) The Viva Voce is meant as an aid to the actual playing at sight, since it comprises questions regarding the key and time signature, pitch and time value of notes, rests, dynamics and other marks of expression. Questions, in other words, which you would have asked yourself in the brief period allowed for looking at the test piece. As it is, you give those answers to the examiner, while gaining time, information and extra marks. In fact, if any of your answers are wrong, the examiner will correct you. Associated Board allows up to half a minute during which candidates may look through and try out any part of the test, before performing it for assessment.

Most experienced teachers set great store by regular Sight Reading and feed their pupils on this wholesome diet. Associated Board, Guildhall, Trinity and London publish specimen papers for all Grades which are obtainable from their publications departments.

SUGGESTED STUDY
Appleby: *Sing at Sight* (OUP)

Bradley & Tobin: *Sightreading Made Easy* (Stainer & Bell)
Cranmer: *Sight-reading for Young Pianists* (Novello)
Davies and Harris: *Improve Your Sight-Reading* (Faber)
Last: *Sight Reading For Today* (Bosworth)
Lee: *Graded Sight Tests* (Lengnick)
Lovelock: *Tests in Sight Reading* (Elkin)

Viva voce

We have already discussed the Associated Board *Viva Voce* requirements for wind players which are part of the Sight Reading test (in 1989 only). The other boards treat these oral questions as a separate section of the practical examination. Guildhall calls it 'General Musicianship' and awards it a maximum of 9 per cent marks, the same as for Sight Reading. The questions for Grades 1 to 3 are related solely to the prepared pieces and concern values of notes and rests, key and time-signatures, and signs, terms and abbreviations in the music. For Grades 4 to 7 there are additional questions on the music performed, on rudiments of music and on the mechanics of the candidate's instrument or vocal technique. For Grade 8 the examiner will play passages from the music performed, and the candidate will be expected to spot deliberate errors and faults in tone production. There are also questions on fingering and pedalling (for pianists), and you are asked to suggest simple pieces for beginners. For 20p you can obtain Guildhall's publication *Questions, Viva Voce, for music examinations, all Grades (complete)*. Trinity allocates 5 per cent maximum marks for their Viva Voce, much less than Guildhall. Questions in all Grades are restricted to the music performed. Grade 1, for example, is concerned with names and duration of notes and time signatures. Grade 2 adds key signatures, Grades 3 and 4 add rests, foreign words and marks of expression, Grade 5 adds modulations, Grade 6 adds form, and Grades 7 and 8 add background details of the pieces and their composers.

London's Viva Voce section carries a maximum of 7 per cent of the total marks, except for their Organ examinations which allocate 15 per cent in Grades 2 to 5, and 5 per cent in Grades 6 to 8. In the lower Grades, the questions are based on the music performed, referring to value of notes and rests, key signatures, musical terms etc, while in Grades 5 to 8 there may be additional questions on such topics as cadences and form (Grade 7) and general questions on the rudiments of music and sonata form (grade 8).

Theory of music

Do not be afraid of the word theory. *It will appear friendly enough once you get to know it.* ROBERT SCHUMANN

Beneath its crusty title there lies an infinite space for the curious to explore. Read about something called an *interrupted cadence*, and you may not much care for it. But experience its effect, as Flutes and Oboes sound their dominant seventh, G – B – F, and then surprisingly yet inexorably glide into the submediant, A – C – E. The untutored ear hardly notices it, but once you are versed in the *theory* of music – a naïve name for *practice* of music – you will relish its effect.

The theory of music is its grammar. Learn the rules, and you have begun to speak the language. Although it is possible to teach yourself, and many adults will just do that, a course of study is called for, which had better be designed and guided by your teacher.

The following is a list of the required areas of study for the examinations from Grade 1 to Grade 8:

Keys and Key Signatures
Time and Time Signatures
Notation and Rests
Musical Signs, Terms and Abbreviations
Intervals
Scales
Form
Ornaments
Chords
Cadences
Harmonization
Transposing
Modulation
Figured Bass
Established Composers and their standard works

Associated Board, Guildhall, Trinity and London provide written examinations in Theory of Music, though Guildhall call theirs 'Rudiments of Music'. Associated Board, Trinity and London offer Grades 1 to 8, while Guildhall precede their Grade 1 with an easier, preliminary paper, but do not go beyond Grade 6. With virtual unanimity, the four boards have decided on a pass mark of 65 per cent (T and L) and 66 per cent (AB and G). Specimen papers are available from their publications departments and should be consulted by student and teacher. Here are a few random requirements:

6/8 time. Triplets. Barring an unbarred phrase. Rhythm of musical phrases in relation to words. (AB, Grade 2)

Leger lines, one above or below the staff. (G, Preliminary)

Writing a simple Piano accompaniment to a given melody, or completing a short piece for three orchestral instruments of which the opening will be given. (T, Grade 8)

Simple questions on musical form as found in vocal music and in dance movement of the classical suite (sarabande, minuet, gavotte). Some knowledge of the composers of such works will be expected. Questions on form will be limited to binary, ternary and rondo form. (L, Grade 6)

The various examination boards are aware of the practical advantages of an understanding of the theory or the rudiments of music. Associated Board insist you have passed Theory Grade 5 before you can take any of the practical Grades 6 to 8. For certain exemptions consult their *Examination Regulations*. Guildhall and Trinity include a written paper in all their practical Grade 8 examinations. For exemptions consult their respective syllabuses.

Luckily, teachers and students can choose from a number of quite excellent publications which provide all the information required, in an entirely practical, occasionally almost mouth-watering manner. Young children are particularly well catered for. You will like:

Chester's Music Puzzles (5 sets) (Chester)
Thompson's Theory Drill Games (3 sets) (Chappell).

The following are also most useful:

Brown: *A Handbook of Musical Knowledge* (T)
Greenish: *The Student's Dictionary of Musical Terms* (Kalmus)
Holst: *An ABC of Music* (OUP)
Huntington: *Pass those Early Grades* (M. Huntington, 10 Marquis Ave, St Johns, Newcastle-on-Tyne)
Huntington: *Pass Your Grade 5 Theory* (see above)
Huntington: *Pass Your Grade 6 Theory and Beyond* (see above)

Macpherson: *The Rudiments of Music* (Kalmus)
Rudiments and Theory of Music (based on the syllabus of the Royal School of Music) (AB)

The next section, too, contains some very useful teaching material and information:

Bastien: *Theory* (Fentone)
Beaven: *Music Theory Makes Sense* (F. Beaven, 603 Walmersley Rd, Bury, Lancs)
Bradley: *Rudiments of Music* (Ricordi)
Chambers Pocket Guide to the Language of Music (Chambers)
Dawe: *New Road to Theory* (Cramer)
Duncan: *A School Theory Exercise Book* (Lengnick)
Edna May Burnham Theory Papers (IMP)
Griffiths: *Theory Flashcards* (Fentone)
Harris: *Lessons in Rudiments* (Forsyth)
Hunt: *The Elements of Music* (Music Sales)
Lee: *A Textbook of Musical Theory and Knowledge* (Lengnick)
Lee: *Music Lover's Examination Question Book* (Banks)
Lovelock: *Test Your Theory* (Elkin)
Lovelock: *Rudiments of Music* (Bell)
Moy: *60 Writing Lessons in Musical Theory* (Lengnick)
Rushford: *Essentials of Elementary Music Theory* (Rubank)
Wharram: *Elementary Rudiments of Music* (Elkin)
Woolley: *Primary Course of Lessons on the Rudiments of Music* (Banks)

Finally, two interesting visual aids:

Computer Practice Program, Grades 2 to 5 (for BBC and Spectrum versions) (T. Kirk, 33 Humber Cresc., Sutton Leach St, St Helens, Merseyside WA9 4HD)
Video: *How To Read Music* (Music Sales)

General musicianship

Building on their musical expertise gained from aural training and from the study of the rudiments of music, candidates can proceed to pit their wits against examination papers in *General Musicianship*. Associated Board offers such an examination in Grades 4 to 7, but this will be replaced in 1990 by an examination in *Practical Musicianship*, covering Grades 1 to 8. Trinity caters for Grades 1, 2, 3, 5, 6 and 8.

In the words of the AB syllabus,

These examinations are designed to widen the general musical under-standing of candidates. Some of the tests involve reproduction from memory and these can be prepared; others will be answered im-promptu. Although they are not intended to be tests in piano playing as such, their performance clearly presupposes a certain keyboard facility.

The examination consists of Keyboard Tests, Sight Singing and Playing, and Aural Tests. In Grade 4, for example, the Keyboard Test requires candidates to play chords and cadences in four-part harmony, to perform a prepared Piano piece of Grade 1 standard, and to transpose it into another key, to transpose a melodic line at sight, and to improvise an answering phrase to a short melody. The Sight Singing Test consists of a short and straightforward diatonic melody, while the Sight Playing comprises a Grade 4 test on an instrument of the candidate's choice. The Aural Test requires recognition of cadences, deciding whether a melody is in a major or minor key, singing or playing the lower part of a two-part phrase, and singing or playing a short phrase after hearing it twice.

If we look at Grade 7, we find the Keyboard Test requires cadential progressions, harmonizing a simple diatonic melody, transposing a four-part passage, continuing a given opening phrase in the style of the music which should include modulation, and playing a three-part vocal score (appr. 8 bars) written in two clefs, G and F. Sight Singing offers a melody of what the syllabus calls 'reasonable difficulty', while the Sight Playing on the candidate's own instrument is a Grade 7 test. The Aural Test is of at least Grade 8 standard.

It can be seen that the General Musicianship tests provide an opportunity for a student to demonstrate his skill as a practical all-round musician equipped with the means of meeting musical challenges. Maximum marks obtainable are as follows:

Keyboard Tests	64%
Sight Singing and Playing	20%
Aural Tests	16%*

Trinity's Musicianship examinations comprise *Performance*, *Musical Perception* and *Composition*. Their syllabus states:

* Specimen Tests for the new Associated Board Practical Musicianship examination are available from April 1989 onwards.

The candidate may take a Musicianship examination playing any instrument (or singing) and may play different instruments in different sections of the examination. In Section 3(b) (Prepared Composition), the candidate may play a solo composition or present a composition for two or three or four performers including himself/herself, the additional player(s) joining the candidate to give the performance.

Grade 1, Performance, demands the playing (any instrument) or singing of a prepared Grade 1 piece, and the sight playing or singing of a Grade 1 test. In the Musical Perception section you are required to clap the rhythm of a piece played by the examiner, to decide whether it is in a major or minor key, and whether it ends with a perfect or plagal cadence. The Composition section calls for the improvisation of an answering phrase to a given one, and the performance of one's own composition lasting no more than two minutes. For Grade 8, the Performance part requires a Grade 8 piece, and a Grade 8 Sight Reading test. In Musical Perception you can choose between playing or singing the lower part of a two-part piece played by the examiner and defining its modulation, or harmonizing a given melody on a keyboard instrument. The Composition section requires extemporizing on a given theme and performing your own composition, between 11 and 12 minutes in length, consisting of at least three movements. Maximum marks obtainable are as follows:

Performance	30%
Musical Perception	30%
Composition	40%

Both the Associated Board and the Trinity examinations in Musicianship should attract candidates who are thinking of music as a career and/or those who are working for a GCSE Music examination. The progressive outlook which has inspired the GCSE syllabuses (see Fact File I on GCSE) is nicely attuned to the graded examinations in Musicianship as outlined above.

SUGGESTED STUDY
Chambers Pocket Guide to Music Forms and Styles (Chambers)
Hunt: *Extemporization for Music Students* (OUP)
Hunt: *Transposition for Music Students* (OUP)
Karolyi: *Introducing Music* (Pelican)
Lang: *Open Score Reading* (Novello)
Lees: *Keyboard Musicianship* (incl. cassettes) (9 Shear Bank Gdns, Blackburn BB1 8AY)

Lovelock: *First Year Harmony* (Elkin)
Lovelock: *Form in Brief* (Elkin)
Musicianship for Students (Novello)
Musicianship Training according to Kodály Principles (3 cassettes) (Sound News)
Paynter: *All Kinds of Music* (OUP)
Stuart-Duncan: *General Musicianship* (Lengnick)

Concert going

The courses in Aural Training, Sight Reading, Theory and General Musicianship which we have discussed all contribute to your musical development. But there is one further aspect to progress in music, one which is not examinable – regular, informed listening.

When Bach was a young man, he tramped 300 miles from Arnstadt to Lübeck, to hear the Danish organist Buxtehude. He stayed for four weeks, practising at night what he had learnt during the day. Today he would obtain a gramophone record, tape or compact disc and learn everything he wanted to learn by listening, not once but as many times in succession as he desired. Diderik Buxtehude, in his organ loft in Lübeck, would hardly have complied with young Johann Sebastian's entreaties for one encore after another. No period in history has been as fortunate as ours, when it comes to listening opportunities. It is this very superabundance which makes some of us neglectful of its blessings, just as local people often have no use for their art gallery which thousands come from all over the world to visit. Radio 3 and, increasingly, TV Channel 4 present you, over a period of time, with the chance of listening to substantial samples from our musical heritage, while at the same time introducing contemporary trends to all who care about the survival of music.

If you possibly can, supplement your home listening with live performances. Not even the highest of hi-fi can match the thrill of attending an event face to face with the artists. The *recorded* sound will often approach perfection, due to sophisticated studio gadgetry and to the countless repetitions of quite small sections of the music, which is part of the recording process. But to be there when Alfred Brendel plays a Schubert Sonata, or when the Birmingham Symphony Orchestra performs Mahler's Second Symphony, or when the curtain rises on Verdi's *Aida*, is tantamount to sharing the stimulation, the spontaneity and also the risks of a live performance with its performers.

Quite a few potential devotees are deterred from attending concerts or operas because of the mechanics involved in finding out what is on, and in obtaining tickets. Many young people, students, unemployed and senior citizens are unaware of reduced prices for attending concerts etc. Others are frightened by the idea of having to listen to an opera sung in a foreign language. The following hints may be useful:

1 Consult the newspapers for details of concerts, operas and ballets. These appear on Saturdays in such publications as *The Times, Daily Telegraph, Independent, Guardian,* and on Sundays in the *Sunday Times, Observer* and *Sunday Telegraph.* Your public library also displays information, frequently in the form of monthly bulletins.

2 Once you have decided on your event, book a seat either in person, by phone or in writing. Addresses and phone numbers are on the advertising pages.

3 Many orchestras, societies and opera companies run concession schemes. Query at time of booking. Here are just a few current examples of what might be on offer at any given time:

- *English National Opera,* London Coliseum. *Family Package:* Buy 2 seats at full price in Stalls or Dress Circle and one or two tickets for children under 16 for £6.50 each.

- *City of Birmingham Symphony Orchestra.* Join the *Junior CBSO Society* and obtain concert tickets at half price.

- *Hallé Orchestra,* Manchester Free Trade Hall. Groups of 10 or more students obtain half price tickets.

- *Scottish National Orchestra,* Edinburgh, Usher Hall. *Special Concerts:* all children's tickets £2.50, senior citizens £2.50 for any seat not sold by 2 pm on day of concert.

- *Robert Mayer Concerts,* London, Royal Festival Hall. £7.00 or £8.50 for 6 Saturday morning concerts. Contact Elizabeth Russell, BBC Yalding House, 156 Gt Portland St, London W1N 6AJ (Tel. 01 927 4523).

- *Youth Makes Music.* 14- to 30-year-olds can obtain tickets for opera, concerts and dance at a reduction of about 50 per cent. Contact Alicia Carroll, Youth & Music, 78 Neal St, London WC2H 9PA (Tel. 01 379 6722).

- *Youth Makes Music North East.* Same conditions and concessions as above. Contact Marj Barton, Youth & Music North East, c/o Northern Centre for Contemporary Art, 15–17 Grange Terrace, Sunderland SR2 7DF (Tel. Wearside 5655212).

The above list is by no means exhaustive, and details may change from season to season.

You will get more enjoyment and enlightenment out of your concert going, if you do a little homework beforehand. Suppose your programme features the Second Symphony by Sibelius. You can, of course, buy the evening's programme, which may cost rather more than it is worth, but which gives an account of the music you are about to hear. By the time you have read the first few lines, however, the conductor may well have walked on and you will have to stop reading. Far better to make use of the resources of your public library. Take out a record/cassette/disc of the symphony, and with it a book which describes the work in detail, together with a miniature score if you are advanced enough to profit from it. There are several concert goers' guides on the market, and your library is bound to stock some of them:

Biancolli & Mann: *The Analytical Concert Guide* (Cassell)
Downes: *Everyman's Guide to Orchestral Music* (Dent)
Ferguson: *Masterworks of the Orchestral Repertoire* (University of Minnesota)
Hopkins: *Talking About Symphonies* (Heinemann)
Newmarch: *The Concert Goer's Library* (OUP)
Shore: *Sixteen Symphonies* (Longmans)
Spaeth: *Guide To Great Orchestral Music* (Modern Library)
Tovey: *Essays in Musical Analysis* (OUP)
Warburton: *Analyses of Musical Classics* (Longmans)
Westerman: *Concert Guide* (Thames & Hudson)

Another source of information is a biography of the composer in question. These are arranged alphabetically on the library shelves, and a brief consultation will enable you to choose the most promising one. Reading about the symphony and listening to it, with or without score, prepares you for the concert. Do all concert goers do this, you may ask. Alas, no. If they did, their involvement in the evening's music would be even greater. If you were to approach your Sibelius concert in the manner just outlined, his Second Symphony could be yours for ever. Likewise, going to the opera calls for a certain amount of homework, especially if the work is presented in its original language, which may be Italian, German, Russian or French. The Royal Opera House Covent Garden has devised a procedure which keeps its audiences informed by means of *surtitles*, i.e. an abbreviated English translation which is projected, much like subtitles on TV, but high above the action on the stage. Again, it is suggested that you obtain a recording of the opera in question, which normally includes a libretto in English, together with a vocal score. The stories of most operas in the current repertoire can be found in these books:

Kobbé's Complete Opera Book (Putnam)
Newman: *Opera Nights* (Putnam)
Newman: *More Opera Nights* (Putnam)
Newman: *Wagner Nights* (Putnam)
Peltz & Lawrence: *Metropolitan Opera Guide* (Modern Library)
Rosenthal & Warrack: *Concise Oxford Dictionary of Opera* (OUP)

Holiday courses

One of the greatest thrills which corporate music making provides is available to you when you participate in a holiday course or music camp. These are held throughout the year, and well over 300 will have taken place during the last twelve months. Their scope is truly all-embracing. The following random selection of current courses makes its point:

Playing the Lute and Guitar	Conducting Clinic
Flute Course	Recorder Playing
Cello Technique	Viola Playing
Brass Enthusiasts	National Children's Orchestra
Woodwind Repair	Baroque and Classical Oboe
Bow Rehairing	and Bassoon
Jazz Workshop	Horn Workshop
Clarinet Course	Woodwind Weekend
Preparing for Grade 5 Theory	Chamber Music for Amateurs
Opera Workshop	Enjoyment of Opera
Early Music Singing	Everyone Can Sing
Saxophone Workshop	Family Singing Week
Bach Cantata Weekend	Viol Consorts
You and Your Violin	Percussion Weekend
Singing For Fun	Wind Chamber Music
Wind Band	Oboe Clinic
Interpretation of Lieder	French Choral Music

Holiday courses frequently feature tuition in small groups, with ample individual coaching, full rehearsals and playing sessions with all participants, and opportunities for students to mix with and play alongside professional tutors. Addresses of course organizers can be found in:

British Music Education Yearbook (Rhinegold Publ.), under 'Recreational Courses'.
British Music Yearbook (Rhinegold Publ.), under 'Part-Time Training and Recreational Courses'.

Details also appear in the monthly journal *Music Teacher*, which publishes a very comprehensive list early every year.

A final word of warning to teachers, parents and adult students: avoid disasters! The author has had to deal with quite a few candidates who had studied the wrong music, usually through working from an out-of-date syllabus. Associated Board regulation 21(b) states:

> Any candidate offering a wrong piece or study or not being prepared to perform the whole of the work specified in the current syllabus for the Grade under examination will be liable to disqualification.

Having to enforce the regulation is a distressing experience. Another frequent cause for falling short of a pass mark must be attributed to the student's or the teacher's neglect of one or more areas of the examination. This can happen when a person other than the instrumental or singing teacher is responsible for entering the candidate for a particular examination, and there is insufficient liaison. For example, a school's music teacher enters a dozen instrumentalists who are taught by one or more visiting teachers. If the latter assume that their responsibility ends with teaching the examination pieces, they may totally neglect Scales and Arpeggios, or Aural Tests or Playing at Sight. This can also happen where no clear understanding has been reached between private teachers and parents.

Mr XYZ, a fine Piano teacher, wrote the following letter of complaint to the examination board for whose Grade 5 he had entered his pupil:

> Matthew W. has obtained practically top marks in all his pieces. He and his parents were shattered when they heard that the boy had failed his examination. Surely this is a ghastly error. Please investigate.

Matthew had indeed scored highly for performing his pieces. Unfortunately, he was unprepared for Aural Tests, Sight Reading and Scales and Arpeggios and, gathering very few marks in these departments, scored a total of 3 marks below pass. But for inadequate communication between

Matthew's teacher and his parents, he could have been properly prepared and might have passed with merit or higher.

To end on a happy note, Matthew emerged unscathed. Twelve months later he passed Grade 7 Piano with 92 per cent.

POSTSCRIPT
'When I give advice to my pupils, I tell them they can do one of three things:

    (a) accept it blindly – bad!
    (b) reject it blindly – bad, but not so bad!
    (c) think over a third course for themselves – good!'

Ralph Vaughan Williams

4 PRACTISING

*An ounce of practice is
worth a pound of preaching.*

OLD PROVERB

'Practising bores me more than words can tell,' writes Richard G., Piano, aged fourteen, in response to requests for comments on this crucial aspect of preparing for an examination. He continues, 'In fact, I would have to be Charles Dickens to describe what it does to me.'

This is more sad than amusing. Richard's attitude suggests that his teacher had failed to *enlighten* and to *motivate* her pupil. She could have tried to *motivate* him by linking the routine of practising the Piano with Richard's routine of practising roller skating (of which the teacher was aware). A few words might have sufficed to establish the link between the two activities, and for Richard to accept the desirability of progressing through practice. The teacher might even jettison the word *practice* altogether and substitute the more suggestive *training*. *Practice* can suggest imposed drill, monotony, daily round, tedium. *Training* implies voluntary exertion, advance, breakthrough, conquest. Some teachers have, in fact, devised alternatives for the term *practising*, usually in accordance with the student's nature, such as *studying*, *pioneering*, *developing*, *maturing*, *advancing* and *perfecting*. It would have contributed to Richard's *enlightenment*, had his teacher shown him *how* to practise, instead of merely advising him to 'go to page four, second line'.

The wise teacher demonstrates the actual process of practising. She discusses the work in hand with her pupil, and together they map out a practice campaign for the following week. They agree on sections which are in special need of attention. The teacher indicates how to tackle such problem areas. She impresses upon her students the benefits of repetition, by playing, say, a couple of bars very slowly, even tentatively, over and over again, each time just a fraction more assured until, after ten minutes or so, the two bars sound more proficient. Those are ten minutes well spent, for only through witnessing a professional's way will he learn what practising means.

Here is a suggested outline of one week's Piano practice. Other instruments can adopt the same principles.

DAY 1	*First Piece*	problem bars 6–9	10 mins	(a)
	Second Piece	bars 1–8	5 mins	(b)
	Improvisation	second piece, simplified for beginners	7 mins	(c)
	Scales/Arp.	D major, both hands, legato	5 mins	(d)
	Sight Reading	No. 1, right through without stopping or correcting	3 mins	(e)
DAY 2	*First Piece*	problem bars 28–33	10 mins	
	Second Piece	bars 6–16	5 mins	
	Improvisation	first piece, new melodic line to existing bass	7 mins	
	Scales/Arp.	D major, both hands, staccato	5 mins	
	Sight Reading	No. 2 (as before)	3 mins	
DAY 3	*Second Piece*	bars 14–24	15 mins	
	Improvisation	Theme: *Contrasts*	7 mins	
	Scales/Arp.	D major, both hands, crescendo going up, decrescendo going down	5 mins	
	Sight Reading	No. 3 (as before)		
DAY 4	*First Piece*	problem bars 40–43	15 mins	
	Improvisation	Theme: *Echoes*	7 mins	
	Scales/Arp.	D major, both hands, decrescendo going up, crescendo going down	5 mins	
	Sight Reading	No. 1 (silent study)	3 mins	
DAY 5	*First Piece*	problem bars 48–54	10 mins	
	Second Piece	bars 22–32	10 mins	
	Scales/Arp.	D major, right hand *pp*, left hand *f*	5 mins	
	Sight Reading	No. 2 (silent study)	5 mins	
DAY 6	*First Piece*	problem bars 6–9, 28–33, 40–43, 48–54	15 mins	(f)
	Second Piece	bars 1–32	15 mins	

The following principles emerge:

Study and practise two pieces simultaneously. The second could be technically less demanding and need not be an examination piece.

(a) The first piece is practised in *problem areas*, as discussed with the teacher.

(b) The second piece is practised in *overlapping sections*. This avoids the danger of future hesitations between sections practised on consecutive days.

(c) Improvising is an enjoyable pursuit with great potential for developing the student's musical instinct. It should be part of almost every practice session. The suggested themes indicate the twofold value of improvisation. They illuminate the practised pieces in a new manner, and they stimulate the player's imagination. To *play about* with the music, to vary it, to change its speed, its key or time signature, is a good starting point. Other themes which the teacher might suggest are *Ocean, Trains, Birds, Solitude, Factory, Midnight*. This activity breaks the practice period in a pleasantly relaxing way. As Ian W., Violin, aged eight, writes, 'I do like practising because I like to make up tunes at the same time.' Furthermore, Improvisation features prominently in the enlightened GCSE music syllabus.

(d) In practising Scales and Arpeggios, monotony is to be avoided. The Outline suggests one key per week, but with daily thematic changes. This counteracts the danger of mechanical playing, improves the player's technique and brings a whiff of musicality to the drill of running up and down.

(e) It has already been pointed out that Sight Reading is not meant to be faultless at first, and that the student must attempt to play at a steady pace, taking in as many notes as possible, rhythmically as correct as strict timing allows. It is now suggested that in two out of the five Sight Reading sessions the student should study the piece mentally only, with due regard to details. The effect of such silent, painstaking study may well be reflected in fewer errors during the coming weeks.

(f) The final session before the next lesson is devoted entirely to the two pieces, refining the week's achievements.

The given timing is, of course, flexible. It suggests major attention to one piece every day, and approximately as much time for Improvisation as for Scales and Arpeggios plus Sight Reading. The total of thirty minutes is ample up to Grade 4. Once the student has mastered the art of targeted practising, his new half hours can be twice as long as his previous whole hours.

Since practising normally takes place at home, communication between teacher and parents is essential. A notebook is preferable to scribbling messages in the margins of the student's printed music. Taking the earlier Outline as an example, the relevant page in the Practice Notebook might look like this:

March 1st to 6th

First Piece	Bars 6–9, 28–33, 40–43, 48–54.
Second Piece	Bars 1–32.
Improvisation	*Contrasts; Echoes*; simplified version of second piece; new melody for first piece.
Scales/Arp.	D major, both hands: legato; staccato;

$$< \ > ; > \ < ;$$

	right hand *pp* and left hand *f*.
Sight Reading	Nos 1, 2 and 3, including silent study.

Students react differently in their attitude towards practising. An oboist, a French Horn player, a harpist may love the sound of his instrument so much that he looks forward to every practice session. As Richard W., aged eleven, writes, 'I do enjoy praxing because I like the sound of my Viola, and praxing makes me better.'

The majority of students, however, depend on regular team support. Having discussed the teacher's part, we will now indicate how the student's family can help.

Find the most suitable location for your child's undisturbed practice. The ideal place is a well ventilated, quiet room, which does not act as a thoroughfare for other members of the household. It is efficiently lit, but not with spotlights. Its temperature is around 65°F, and it offers storage facilities for the student's music and accessories. There should be a clock, mirror, music stand (for non-pianists), footstool (for guitarists), a suitable writing surface and, if possible, a metronome.

As soon as practicable after each lesson, mother (or father or other adult) and child should hold their weekly discussion, perhaps in the shape of a *working tea*, where the next six days' effort is mapped out. The adult should, however, beware of acting as a second teacher. Her role within the student's support team is an auxiliary one. She should be available to listen to the child's practice, when asked. She should be unstinting in her praise and encouragement, whenever the occasion warrants it (and sometimes when it does not). In the case of a young string player, it would be an excellent plan for one member of the family

151

to take a consultation lesson in tuning the instrument, so that the child need not struggle against an out-of-tune Violin or Cello. However slow the progress and however crude the beginner's initial sounds, do not refer to them as *noise*, and cajole the rest of the family to abstain likewise. Try to enjoy the child's practice. Both of you are in the position of a sculptor contemplating a block of marble in which he visualizes his as yet invisible work of art. Share the analogy with your child. *

When is the best time to practise? Much depends on the household routine, but it is advisable to arrange for practice to take place at the same time every day. Ideally, this should be a time when other members of the family, friends or neighbours are not indulging in some particularly pleasurable activities. It should also be a time when the student is fresh in mind and body. This could suggest an early morning period, before breakfast, as the most suitable one.

Where the student is a pianist, a further point must be considered. If at all possible, arrange for your child to see and try a grand piano, even if only for a few minutes. It is not unusual for young children to panic when they enter the examination room which features a grand piano instead of the familiar upright. When examining a six-year-old pianist, the author had to comfort the boy who had broken into floods of tears the moment he saw the big black monster, so unlike the gentle companion he had grown up with.

Students, especially older ones, may wish to consider the following guidelines:

- Since practising involves a great deal of repetition, never repeat anything automatically. Aim at some improvement, however minute, at each reiteration. Put your ears firmly in charge. Let them establish a perfect sound picture of the passage you are about to practise, and bid your fingers or lips to comply.
- When your practised music approaches performance standard, regard your fingers as members of an orchestra, with yourself as their conductor. Make the performance an interesting one. Let them execute your instructions concerning dynamics, phrasing, pitch and rhythm. Study your music away from the instrument, as a conductor studies his score. Endeavour to hear, in your mind, an impressive performance of your music. Then go back to your instrument and live up to it.

How do professional artists approach their practising, and what advice have they to offer? The author asked several renowned musicians for their opinions. Here are their messages for the reader.

* A useful parents' guide is *The Art of Practising* by P. Lee (Hamilton Brook Publications).

Peter Katin

This outstanding pianist has made a special study of the topic and has reached conclusions which are to some extent based on medical research:

> It is not wise to force the concentration for too long when practising, as the brain's ability to concentrate operates on a rapid on/off sequence, akin to A.C. electrical current. The natural span of concentration is in fact no more than about 20 minutes, although performers have increased this to an hour. After this time a short break should be taken, and even a few minutes' walk should be all that is needed to re-charge the brain, but one should *not* during this break remain at the instrument, or in the case of singers, they should not sing at all at this time.

Moura Lympani

This concert pianist, beloved by generations of admirers, recommends:

> Give frequent performances to yourself when practising.

This is in happy accord with the earlier recommendation on p. 152. Moura Lympani continues:

> Start practising slowly. Set your metronome a little faster every day.

Used wisely, the metronome can be a powerful ally, but do not become its slave. Moura Lympani's final proposal is brief and heart-warming:

> Talk to yourself.

Precisely! Tell yourself how to make that E flat major arpeggio more even. Tell yourself what is still wrong with those octave leaps in one of your pieces. Needle yourself into corrective action. When you have solved a tricky problem, speak highly of yourself.

Sir Colin Davis

The former director of the Royal Opera, Covent Garden, is now the chief conductor of one of the finest West German orchestras. He submits:

How to practise very much depends on who is at home and what support you get.

A most important point. Many children like to practise in such a way that they can be overheard. Or, as Kay R., Bassoon, aged eleven, puts it, 'If someone listens, I like practising. If not I don't.'
From one eminent conductor to another.

Bryan Fairfax

Having trained numerous students to become expert conductors, Bryan Fairfax puts his finger on a problem which can obstruct the practising process:

> Students are imbued with the idea that music is a subject for an *inspirational* approach, but the painstaking *analytical* approach which is needed for careful practising does not always appeal.

Avoid this dilemma. Stick to *analysing* your practice procedure, and reserve the *inspirational* aspect for performing. Fairfax continues:

> There is no alternative to slow – extremely slow – tempi. I am a great believer in the metronome, but students possess such an instrument mainly to find out *how fast* a piece should be. I have been told by musicians who had overheard Cherkassky, Oistrakh and Casals practising in hotel rooms, of the exceptionally slow tempi they adopted. Only at a really slow speed can one analyse the gymnastics of finger, wrist, arm etc.

Antony Hopkins

Here is sterling advice, coming from a celebrated composer, conductor, pianist, author, lecturer and regular broadcaster.

> Always practise *beyond* a difficulty, so that when you return to the actual context it seems easier. For instance, practise leaps an octave further than written, parallel runs with your hands crossed etc. Isolate a problem by practising one note each side of it, then two, then three and so on.

Finally, words of wisdom from a beginner and from one at the top of his profession. Caroline D., Violin, aged ten:

I adore practising, because I adore the music.

Julian Lloyd Webber

In the early days it is important to have goals to aim at, and in this respect examinations can be a great spur. Basically, it is a matter of loving the music enough to want to play it better.

POSTSCRIPT
'Practice, inability to, is my single greatest musical weakness. It has led me to atrocious first performances. I am blessed/cursed with a good ear and I tend to coast on it. I have the distinction, still unique, of having been expelled from the Peabody Conservatory of Music in Baltimore.'

Larry Adler, Harmonica virtuoso, in a letter to the author

5 EXAM NERVES

Mitte hanc de pectore
curam (Dismiss this
anxiety from your mind).

VIRGIL

As the examination date approaches, candidates are likely to anticipate the looming event with a mixture of apprehension and buoyancy. It is a healthy blend, provided neither ingredient is allowed to eclipse the other. Buoyancy must not lapse into carelessness, nor apprehension into panic.

'I get so nervous in the exam room,' writes Mary B., Piano, aged sixteen, 'my fingers turn to jelly.' But fourteen-year-old Hamish M., Trumpet, confesses, 'When I took my Grade 5 I went rigid with nerves.' Can *nerves* really make one person go limp, and ossify another? Mandy R., Flute, eighteen, puts yet another, highly significant point. 'I have never really been nervous before, but all my friends have. So when I played my Grade 8 pieces, I thought of what my friends had said, and I became very nervous indeed.'

Let us examine the nature of nervousness and its manifestations, before discussing the means of defeating it. The colloquial term *nerves* covers such phenomena as fear of the unknown, self-distrust and general apprehension. These are mental states which can trigger off a number of effects, such as tension (Hamish going rigid), or alarm (Mary's fingers turning to jelly), or sudden blind spots (Mandy landing herself with her friends' nerves). *Fear of the unknown* troubles the person who is unsure of the situation. *Self-distrust* generally troubles the person who is unsure of himself. *Sudden blind spots* are trespassing red herrings.

The first, fear of the unknown, presents no problem, provided the examination procedure has been thoroughly explained and rehearsed. The reader will participate in just such a rehearsal when turning to the next chapter, 'The Day'. Not much, however, can be done about self-distrust, at least not at the run-up stage to the examination. Its cause is obvious. It stems from the candidate's lack of competence in one or more of the requirements and should never have been permitted to arise. It has been advocated before that the candidate should be at least half a

156

grade ahead of the standard expected, not only in his playing, but also in all other departments. He will then be able to approach the examination day in a confident frame of mind, since there will be no anxiety over technical obstacles. On the contrary, the candidate will be free to concentrate on the *musical* aspect of the examination. The following messages to the reader from two renowned performers should convince the doubtful. Norbert Brainin:

It is my experience that the mastering of certain problems of instrumental technique automatically overcomes 'nerves', and there are no short cuts.

James Galway:

You don't get nervous if you know what you're doing.

This leaves us with the third cause of nervousness, general apprehension and its retinue, those sudden blind spots. They often manifest themselves in a vague state of agitation, possibly accompanied by a heightened pulse rate. This state of mind is quite natural just before an important event, such as an enquiry into our competence and resourcefulness. You can make it work for you, as long as you are not misled by those who believe this readiness for the fray is *nervousness*. It is not. Shakespeare analyses that state of electrification of mind and body in *Henry V*, when the royal war lord Henry addresses his soldiers:

> In peace there's nothing so becomes a man
> As modest stillness and humility;
> But when the blast of war blows in our ears,
> Then imitate the action of the tiger;
> Stiffen the sinews, summon up the blood,
> Disguise fair Nature with hard-favour'd rage;
> Then lend the eye a terrible aspect;
> Let it pry through the portage of the head
> Like the brass cannon. . . .
> Now set the teeth and stretch the nostril wide;
> Hold hard the breath. . . .
> I see you stand like greyhounds in the slips,
> Straining upon the start. The game's afoot;
> Follow your spirit; and upon this charge,
> Cry, God for Harry, England, and Saint George.

In modern parlance, and bereft of its poetry, this could be summarized:

It is all very well to take things easy when there is no war on. But here we are, facing the enemy. Can you feel the adrenalin* rising in your veins? You can? Let it lead you to victory!

In his assessment of the situation, Shakespeare has found a powerful ally in Julian Lloyd Webber, consummate cellist, to whom the author is indebted for the following contribution to this chapter:

It would be a curious artist who never suffered from nervousness, as this would surely imply a lack of feeling for the sense of occasion, which there always must be. So the question is not how to 'get over' nerves but how to control them and even make them work to your advantage. I believe nerves can be made to work for, rather than against you – that extra flow of adrenalin sharpening the reflexes and giving each performance a special edge. The best way of controlling nervousness is the most obvious: you should lose yourself totally in the music, so that the body becomes merely a channel for it to flow through. If the mind is given completely to something outside the physical body, nerves disappear. There will naturally be days when nervousness seems to be getting the upper hand, but during my college days I learned one or two specific ways of dealing with it. For example, when my right hand began shaking and the bow bounced all over the strings, I would immediately focus attention on my left-hand fingers, and I'd forget about the bow, and it would start to behave properly again. There may be many such tricks for dealing with nerves and doubtless every performer must develop his own.

Let us turn once more to Shakespeare, for there is further advice in that passage for the music student.

Imitate the action of the tiger.

In other words, if you *look* like a tiger, you may convince first yourself, then everybody else, that you *are* a tiger. Or, for our present purpose, let your body coax your mind into experiencing the emotion suggested by

---

* Adrenalin: a substance which is made inside your body when you are angry, nervous or excited, and causes your heart to beat faster and gives you more energy (*Collins Cobuild English Language Dictionary*).

your mute body language. When about to play some cheerful music, look cheerful first. Your eyes will sparkle, and so will the music (and the examiner). Conversely, if your music is pensive, do not be afraid to show this in your bearing. Next time you eat out, watch the waiter. If he sulks, he probably dislikes his job, but his scowl merely aggravates his resentment. Let him profit from his colleague whose sunny countenance either reflects his job satisfaction or, more likely, calls it forth. This commonsensical truth has long been recognized. Hence the saying, *putting a brave face* on something. Reflect on King Henry's psychologically sound exhortations:

Stiffen the sinews.

Summon up the blood.

Lend the eye a terrible aspect.

Set the teeth.

Stretch the nostril wide.

Hold hard the breath.

And then he draws the accurate conclusion:

Follow your spirit.

It worked for Harry's yeomen. It will work for you.

More can be done about *nervousness* before it ever shows its unbecoming head. Many students, young and mature, experience what they might describe as *stage fright*, when called to play or sing in front of the examiner. Preventive measures should be taken, long before the event, to counteract this unpleasant sensation. Candidates contemplating a graded examination should have frequent opportunities of performing to an audience which contains unfamiliar faces. Many teachers recognize this. They are to be applauded for organizing pupils' concerts, a time-consuming, often unpaid but vital extension of their teaching practice. Such concerts can be either formal or informal. The audience consists of families and friends of the performers. If the occasion is a formal one, a small hall may have been hired, with the object of providing the performers with the experience of playing and singing to an audience, of coping with strange surroundings and acoustics, and of displaying their platform manners. If these have been discussed beforehand between teacher and pupils, they should promote an easy, relaxed attitude on the part of the performer. This will include an unembarrassed smile with which he greets his audience and, where applicable, his accompanist. Such essential platform training will pay dividends later, when the candidate faces the examiner.

On no account should such concerts be used to show off the achievements of one *prize pupil*, to the possible detriment of the other students. All items should be fairly brief and offer a variety of moods and styles. As an added bonus, the teacher may herself give a short performance, or she could invite a fellow professional to share the platform.

Informal concerts are often held in the teacher's studio. Here pupils can perform not only as soloists, but in pairs and in groups – pianist accompanying violinist, string players forming a trio or quartet, and two, three or even four pianists playing four-handed, six-handed or eight-handed music (think of it, forty fingers!). Whatever the artistic achievements of such pupils' concerts, the experience gained is priceless, while another weapon has been forged for the battle against nervousness. Or, in Sir Colin Davis's words:

> If there is sufficient exposure, from childhood days, this problem doesn't seem to be so overwhelming, but these are early days for me to be so sure of myself. Ask me again in another ten years, if I am still here.

Further steps can be taken to neutralize disagreeable symptoms of nervousness. Robert Farley, the prodigious young trumpeter, offers this advice from the performer's position, under the headings 'Situation' and 'Occasion':

> By Situation I mean things like temperature, where you sit etc. For example, if you stand up to play 'The trumpet shall sound', and you are in a cold church with a cold instrument which is not up to pitch, this leads to panic. Also, if you sit in an awkward position in the orchestra where you can't see the conductor, this too can cause avoidable alarm. The answer is to think of these problems before they come up, e.g. keep the instrument warm, and make sure you are in a good position to see the conductor.
>
> Occasion: this category is harder to deal with. It involves events that don't present their attendant problems until it's too late. For instance, you have done all your practising, have had a final rehearsal with the orchestra, and it is only when you go on stage that you get the jitters. What to do about it? The best way is a pre-emptive one. It

involves putting yourself under pressure beforehand, by standing up in front of people to play (or speak). You have to be prepared to fall on your face several times, before you achieve your goal. For brass and woodwind players, a dry mouth is the most common source of nerves. So take a glass of water on to the stage to keep the mouth moist. In an emergency, bite your tongue when it dries up. The best answer, however, I have found is oxygen. When I get tense I concentrate on my breathing. Taking a couple of really deep breaths before I play, helps to take the mind off any looming problems.

As a player or singer, you have learned to control your fingers, your lips, your breathing. Controlling your nerves is just as achievable, and only you yourself can do it. Guard against advice such as given by a medical practitioner, at a recent conference on tension in performing, who advocated the use of a beta-blocking drug to be taken by nervous performers. This may well work, and there may be no significant side-effects. But the cost is prohibitive, not in pounds and pence, but in the drug taker's admission of his failure to be in charge. For in fending off nervousness, the beta-blocker may also block spontaneity, excitement and the willingness to take risks – all hallmarks of a genuine musician.

Robert Farley suggests deep breathing as a shock absorber. Consider setting aside a few minutes every day for supplementing your practice routine with these easy exercises:

- Sit somewhere comfortable. Close your eyes and go all floppy. Breathe slowly in and out, in and out. Think of nothing at all. Concentrate on your breathing alone.

- The previous exercise had *two* beats to the bar. This has *three*. Flop as before. Now breathe in, hold your breath for a few seconds, then breathe out. Think of a very lazy waltz, danced by two tortoises. One: in – two: hold – three: out.

- Many musicians suffer from aches in their necks and shoulders. Here is a counter-measure. Sit or stand, arms by your sides. Breathe in, while raising your shoulders up to your ears. Breathe out while allowing your shoulders to drop. Repeat several times.

Teachers, parents and students may be interested in the activities of the *International Society for the Study of Tension in Performance*. The society is concerned about the 'debilitating effects of excess anxiety and tension experienced by performers'. It promotes research, holds conferences and provides an advisory service for its members. Contact:

Audrey Lyndon, ISSTIP, Gipsy Hill Centre, Kingston Polytechnic, Kingston upon Thames KT2 7LB (Tel. 01 549 1141).

SUGGESTED STUDY
Green & Gallwey: *The Inner Game of Music* (Pan)
Grindea: *Tension in the Performance of Music* (Kahn & Averill)
Reubart: *Anxiety and Musical Performance* (Da Capo Press)

POSTSCRIPT
'I know about nervous tension, but I'm enough of a pro to be nearly immune to it. I *am* nervous when debuting a new work, the composer in the audience. It is useful to relax before a performance. Whichever way suits is the best way. Emil Coué made a fortune getting rich ladies to say aloud, "Every day in every way I'm getting better and better and better." Even that is good if it works. It wouldn't work for me, I'd start to giggle.'

Larry Adler, in a letter to the author

6 THE DAY

*The night is far spent, the
day is at hand: let us
therefore cast off the works
of darkness, and let us put
on the armour of light.*

(Rom. 13:11)

At last! Provided the Entry Form has been filled in correctly. Has it?

Teacher or parent or mature student has to post this form, together with the entrance fee, some six weeks prior to the examination period. The Entry Form (Associated Board) requires name, address and telephone of *applicant*. This is where many have spoilt the form and need to write for another one, for they mistakenly entered the name of the *candidate* in those little blue boxes which harbour everything you fill in, one letter per box. The *applicant*, remember, is the person who takes responsibility for *entering* the candidate; who fills in the form and who will receive confirmation of entry with relevant details and, eventually, the Mark Form and the Certificate. There are also boxes marked 'Code of Centre for Examination'. These codes are shown in the Associated Board Regulations under 'Examination Centres and Honorary Local Representatives' (with phone numbers). Make use of the latter's knowledge, if help is required.

The *candidate's* name, as it appears on the Entry Form, will later be shown on the candidate's Mark Form. Since the examiner has to fill this in, either before the examination day or while waiting for the candidate to be shown in, restrict forenames to a minimum. By the time the examiner has entered Annemarie Veronica Marigold Thistlethwaite in the 2½ inches of space provided, he* will not only have made a mess of the form, but Annemarie has been kept waiting. Other information required is the Subject Code (e.g. Piano – Ol, as shown in right-hand top corner of Entrance Form), Grade Number (in arabic numerals!), Theory

---

* To avoid the clumsy *he/she* business, it is proposed to call *all* examiners *he*, although lady examiners are employed as follows: AB 26%, G 44%, T 18%, L 20%.

Qualification (Theory Grade 5 or above must have been passed for all practical Grades 6, 7 and 8), and details of Blind Candidates (where applicable). As for the examination date, you are offered some limited choice. There are boxes for 'Saturdays inconvenient', for 'preferred week' and for 'last available date', although the Board reserves the right to overrule your request.

Let us now launch into a mock examination, beginning with the previous day. You have been given the address of the place at which to present yourself. This is either a private house, a public venue or a school. The former could be a music teacher's studio or some other private home which offers such amenities as a suitable waiting area, toilet facilities, low noise level and a fair-sized examination room which often contains a grand piano. The public venue may be a church hall or meeting place, with facilities similar to those at the private home. In either case, an official steward will be at hand to receive and look after the candidates. These are almost always experienced, sympathetic persons whose shoulders are for crying upon if necessary.

Where the examination centre is a school, matters are a little more involved. If the candidate is a member of that particular school, he will be familiar with the whole set-up, and he might even have the use of a practice room before his examination. It can be intimidating, however, for someone from another school to enter a strange building, find his bearings, possibly neglecting to ask where the toilets are, and experience a noise pattern different from the one he is used to. When examining in schools, the author has met some exceptionally efficient arrangements, with prefects posted at the gates, making strangers feel at home, quiet waiting rooms with comics, biscuits, soft drinks and meticulous stewarding. He has also experienced the opposite.

Whichever address you have been given, *go there before the examination day*. If it is in your vicinity, time your unhurried walk, but make alternative travel arrangements in case of adverse weather. Check on availability and reliability of public transport and allow extra time. If you go by car, find out about parking at your appointed time, again allowing for walking from the parked car to the examination place. Once you know how to get there and when to begin your journey, you will have saved yourself needless apprehension on the day.

You should have been informed of your examiner's name. If not, ask the local representative. To enter the examination room with a smile and his name on your lips will be pleasant for both of you.

Now is the time to prepare a check list of everything you are planning to take on tomorrow's trip. It might look like this:

Instrument and Case   Footstool
Music Stand*   Printed Music†
Pitch Pipe   Book (amusing, for waiting room)
Spares (strings, reeds etc)

Check that your printed music will stand upright at all times. If you have ever folded your music horizontally – a sin almost beyond forgiveness – it is liable to collapse at an inopportune moment. You may be able to fortify it with layers of clear tape along the fold marks and by strengthening its spine.

The evening before the event had best be spent away from your instrument. A visit to the cinema could be arranged, or games and TV at home, or seeing friends. Then a hot bath and bed.

THE DAY
The pleasure of your company is requested at a time not necessarily of your choosing. Broadly, there are six possibilities:

(a) Weekday, early morning;
(b) Weekday, late morning;
(c) Weekday, afternoon;
(d) Saturday, early morning;
(e) Saturday, late morning;
(f) Saturday, afternoon.

Since all good battles are meticulously planned, careful thought should be given as to the most efficient way of organizing the hours before the event. Twenty-eight instrumentalists and singers who had all taken at least three practical examinations were asked how best to spent the time before setting out on the journey to the examination centre. Among the twenty-eight there were three mature students, and the discussion group was augmented by two teachers, a psychologist father and a general practitioner. Allowing for minor disagreements, here are their suggestions:

(a) *Weekday, early morning.* Light breakfast, take apple/sandwich/mints and Thermos (tea/orange juice) and leave well before time. Most

---

* There will be one in the examination room, but you may like to use your own familiar companion.
† Photocopies are not allowed.

candidates agreed that between twenty and thirty minutes should be allowed for traffic or parking problems and *added* to the journey time established on the trial trip. *

(b) *Weekday, late morning*. Indulge in lie-in, enjoy a leisurely but not too heavy breakfast, practise for no more than twenty minutes, and leave with twenty to thirty minutes in hand.

(c) *Weekday, afternoon*. Normal morning school routine, home for lunch (or after school lunch), practise for no more than twenty minutes, and leave with twenty to thirty minutes in hand.

(d) *Saturday, early morning*. As (a) above.

(e) *Saturday, late morning*. As (b) above.

(f) *Saturday, afternoon*. Light activity in the morning, such as walking the dog, swimming, watching TV, reading, lunch, a little practising if time, then leave with at least thirty minutes in hand (Saturday traffic!).

Other recommendations included carrying a mascot (from lucky charm to bear), and – top marks for ingenuity – taking a phone card and spare cash, in case of emergency. Two panel members recalled how a dash to a public phone box and a taxi ride averted disaster, when a Cello in a soft bag was flattened by a bus conductor and, in the other case, when the candidate's car had broken down in a country lane, seven miles from her destination. The first phone call spirited the teacher's Cello to the examination centre ('thank goodness for leaving half an hour early!'), and the second alerted the husband's delivery van.

Consider all proposals and adopt those which suit you best. If you can also find time for the three short exercises outlined on p. 161, so much the better.

Some candidates find it hard to decide what to wear. Do not be fooled by anyone's notion that the examiner is swayed, one way or another, by your appearance. He has seen everything in his time, from dinner suit to leotard, and although he prefers clean fingernails to dirty ones, he will go solely by the musical performance, spruce or unkempt, rags or riches. Wear what makes you feel good. Go for comfort rather than for haute couture. Small girls can look pretty in party frocks, but these can also hinder the free travel of fingers over keys or of bow across strings.

You have now packed everything with the help of your check list and are ready to set out.

* Harpists should arrive at the examination centre thirty minutes early, to allow ample time for tuning.

Will you be accompanied or not? Small children will, of course, be taken on their journey, but older students may prefer their own company, though many derive comfort from the presence of a sympathetic relative, boyfriend or girlfriend. If you are in doubt, ask yourself whether your escort is likely to fuss, or whether it is someone who could cope on a desert island. Whichever mode of transport you choose – public, car or legs – the bicycle and the motorbike had best stay at home.

You have arrived at the examination centre. Your appointment is at 11.37 (those odd times reflect the examiner's tight schedule), and candidates are expected to show themselves ten minutes before their allotted time. It is 11.10, and you have just over a quarter of an hour on your hands. Shall you go in or wait outside? Weigh up the arguments for and against:

	Waiting Room	Outside
Advantages	You can chat to fellow creatures.	You avoid the potentially tense atmosphere of the waiting room.
	You can familiarize yourself with the place.	If the weather is fine, you can stroll and top up with oxygen.
	You have ample time for a snack and a wash, and possibly for a little reading.	If in car, you can open the windows and relax.
Disadvantages	It can be stuffy inside.	You have quite a few things to carry.
	Some other candidate may give you the benefit of his apprehensions.	The weather may be inclement.
	Chatting to others may be the last thing you want to do just now.	If your escort agitates you, you will be better off inside.

Let us assume the time is 11.25, and you have just stepped inside. Let us further propose you are a pianist about to take Grade 3. Your knock at the door is answered by the steward, a kindly lady (or gentleman) who

167

checks your name against her door list and ushers you into the waiting room. She will also show you the 'usual facilities' and ask you whether you wish to warm up your instrument. She then remembers that you are not a trumpeter but a pianist.

This is the time to take the music out of your case and put it in the order in which you are going to play it. Five minutes to go, and you are handed a note. What is this? Never seen one of those before! A *personal message* from the examiner? This is what it says:

```
                  Dear Musical Friend,
          I wish you an enjoyable and successful examination.
          Will you please help me and write the titles of the
          pieces of music you will be performing, in the space
          below:

          1.

          2.

          3.




                  Good wishes and good luck!
                     Rudolph Sabor
```

The author must make a partial retraction. You are only likely to receive one of those notes if he happens to be your examiner. He thinks it might establish some sort of relationship even before we have met. Also, by attending to the details requested, you will have less time to worry about the exam. And it saves the examiner's time. But rest assured: *all* examiners want you to succeed.

11.36: a flautist has emerged from the examination room, and the steward takes you to the door. This is the moment for you to breathe deeply and slowly, and to recall the examiner's name.* At the tinkle of a bell, the steward ushers you in. You smile, enter and bid him good morning.

* If, in spite of all that has been said before about nerves, a sudden terror should grip you at this moment, picture the examiner in his underwear.

THE EXAMINATION

After exchanging a few pleasantries you will be asked to sit at the imposing grand piano (or the less imposing upright). Does the swivel chair need adjusting? If so, the examiner will be happy for you to attend to this. He may even give you a hand. All pianos, whether upright or grand, differ in touch. Your own may be far heavier to the touch than the present one. Do not wait to find out when you play your first scale, but ask whether you may try the Piano for a few seconds. You may, of course. 'Are you quite comfortable? Good. Please play a scale in A major, left hand only.' Your mind registers instantaneously – *left hand, start with little finger*, three sharps, and you are off. Nice and even, two octaves up and two down. 'Now E flat major scale, both hands.' Again, you recall where the flats belong and with which fingers to start. You listen intently to yourself, making both hands play perfectly together. 'C minor scale, please.' You are aware that you can choose between harmonic and melodic minor, and you play the version you have prepared. In all scales your thumb matches your little finger. Though nature had made the former stronger than the latter, here they are equally endowed, neither outdoing the other. After one or two arpeggios, you will be asked to play a scale in contrary motion, possibly in E major. You keep your eyes on your fingers, right eye following right hand up, left eye following left hand down. No, it will not make you cross-eyed. Meanwhile the examiner has been scribbling his comments on the Mark Form. Maximum mark is 21, pass mark 14. This is where careful preparation pays off, and there is no reason why you should not score near 20.

Now your hands are ready for the pieces. Although you may play them in any order, there seems little point in not adhering to the order in the official grade book. We shall take it for granted that your practising has enabled you to play the right notes at the right time. Fine. That means just over 20 marks out of 30 for each of the pieces. But you are after bigger fish. You are not just a player, you are a musician. The performance you now give reflects your musicality. The first piece is an eighteenth-century Sonatina, originally composed for the Clavichord. Your playing evokes its prodding meticulousness. You contrast a forte passage with a piano section. You go for rhythmical accuracy and a clean touch, turning your fingertips into gentle miniature hammers. The second piece is a wistful tone painting of a summer's evening in the forest. So far you have only spoken a few words to the examiner. Now you can let your music talk to him. No need to feel embarrassed – the talk is not about yourself, nor about the exam, but about the swishing of leafy twigs, about the sun plunging leisurely into the young poplars, about a remote nightingale.

Let the examiner share the discoveries you had made when you had found the meaning of the music, the life *behind* the notes. The third piece has an awkward turnover. Wisely, you refrain from asking the examiner to turn the page for you, for he is busy listening and making notes. Some time ago you have neatly cut across the printed page, and before your playing reaches the bottom line you will, at a convenient moment, turn over the top section, revealing the first half of the next page. The examiner does not add a mark for resourcefulness, but he applauds silently.

Playing at Sight. 21 marks are up for grabs, with 14 for a pass. 'You will have a little time in which to look through this piece. You may try any part of it . . . Please start now.'

During the next ten seconds or so you take in the direction 'Lively', the phrase marks and that final chord. Now you are ready. The rhythm is uncomplicated, all crotchets and quavers, with an occasional dotted note. Although one note eluded you and another one may have been wrong, you kept the music moving along. You even managed to make it sound quite attractive.

So far you have harvested a respectable tally of marks. With only the Aural Tests to come, you are able to relax. A pass is pretty certain, even if disaster should strike. But you are going for gold. The examiner asks you to stand by the side of the Piano. 'Listen to these few notes,' he says. 'Sing them after I have played them twice.' Your ears are firmly in charge. You know that he is not testing your voice, but your musical memory, and he will not mind your whistling, as long as you whistle his notes. Your ears register the rising melody which drops at the end. You listen again. Yes, that's it: long, short short long. Easy. The examiner now plays two notes simultaneously. 'Sing the top note, please.' You oblige. How can anyone miss that? But this is not all. Here are another two notes, and you are required to spot the *bottom* note. You remember those aural games you used to play, and your early attempts at listening to a String Trio and concentrating on the Cello. But now you are not so sure. 'Could I possibly hear it again?' No harm in trying. The examiner plays it once more, and you sing the bottom note. He might have given you an extra mark or two, had you been right first time, but you still keep scoring.

'Will you clap this rhythm for me? I shall play it twice.' Listen, but concentrate on the *tune* rather than on the *rhythm*. Then *sing the tune with your hands*. The final test requires you to beat time. You recall the drill: 2 time = down and up; 3 time = down, away (from your body) and up; 4 time = down, across, away and up. The examiner plays a short passage. His first note had no accent. The next one had. After that came two weak beats. So, weak – strong – weak – weak – strong – weak – weak –

strong – weak – weak – strong. Clearly, 3 time. The examiner plays it again. 'Now please beat time.' You beat time, starting on the first strong beat: down, away, up, down, away, up. 'Thank you very much,' he says. 'I enjoyed this. I hope you did.' You gather your belongings and reverse the entrance formalities, except that your smile is now one of relief.

Whatever your Grade, whether you are a string, woodwind or brass player, a singer or percussionist, the procedure will be similar. The following points, though, must be considered.

- Do not scowl when entering the examination room.

- String players below Grade 5 who need help in tuning should have an expert at hand. Where the student's teacher is present, possibly acting as accompanist, there is no problem. The Associated Board examiner will *not* undertake tuning for you.

- Singers, string, woodwind and brass players must make absolutely sure of the services of their accompanist. Apart from several rehearsals, which are essential, the accompanist should meet the candidate at least a quarter of an hour before the examination, for a quick run through. He should be given a note, weeks before the examination, which shows the address and phone number of the centre, travel directions, your own address and telephone, with exact details of the music you are going to perform.

- Examiners, as has been said before, are human. If you are asked anything that is not in the syllabus, do not be afraid to query this. Rehearse some such phrase as, 'Please excuse me, but am I required to know/play/sing this?' The author still counts himself fortunate, for several years ago he examined a Grade 5 clarinettist when, during the Aural Tests, the wind blew over a page of the test book and the candidate was given a Grade 6 question. He did not protest, and he gave the correct answer. But this could easily have gone wrong. You have nothing to lose in asking for a clarification, if in doubt.

- Use the last ten minutes before you are called, to warm up your instrument or voice.

- And remember, don't scowl!

Postscript

Dear Examination Board,

During my recent tour I had to fail a grade 8 student, Miss XYZ. I attached a note to the mark form, stating that this elderly lady should not have been entered by her teacher, because of her physical infirmity (arthritic fingers) which made it quite impossible for her to do herself justice.

Yours sincerely, R.S.

Dear Examiner,

At risk of contravening rules, I am writing to you to thank you for your extreme kindness and understanding towards me, when I made my unsuccessful attempt to pass the grade 8 examination.

I have today received my marks form: all you have written there is so true and understanding; your remarks at the end – 'this candidate's evident musicality' – are to me a complete reward.

I now realise that to a person of 83, a good performance is a physical impossibility; it was, however, a driving force which could not be resisted.

I have enjoyed learning the beautiful music and the discipline of much practice, and with you to give the final word, it has all been well worth while.

My grateful thanks to you.

Yours sincerely, XYZ.

Dear Miss XYZ,

Thank you very much for your kind remarks. Let me say that it was a matter of real and personal regret that I was obliged to abide by the regulations and issue the final marks and verdict, because your innate musicality and real love for the music you were playing was so convincing and touching. I know only too well that fingers and vocal chords are subject to the ravages of time, while love of music can only grow. So we lose in one direction, but gain in the other. It was good having met you.

All good wishes,

Yours sincerely, R.S.

Fact File I
The new GCSE examination

Although this examination falls outside the stated scope of this book, it must be briefly discussed, for its aims are inspired and far-reaching, its contents are student-orientated, and its foreseeable effects on musical education are likely to confer great benefits on pupils and teachers alike.

Whereas the former GCE 'O' Level Music was largely theory-based, with its emphasis on set works, aural tests and rudiments, its successor treats the candidate as a practising musician. It does not penalize the examinee for possible shortcomings in written English, but wants to find out what kind of musician he is. Under the old system you were able to pass without playing a note. Now, instrumental and vocal performances are mandatory. Formerly, a candidate's success or failure depended on his prowess on examination day. Now, his achievements during the preceding school years are also taken into consideration.

This section does not scrutinize the new examination in depth, it merely provides glimpses of some of its features. Syllabuses and specimen papers can be obtained from:

London and East Anglian Group: Publications Dept, East Anglian Examination Board, The Lindens, Lexden Rd, Colchester, Essex CO3 3RL.

Midland Examining Group: Publications Dept, University of Cambridge Local Examinations Syndicate, 1 Hills Rd, Cambridge CB1 2EV.

Northern Examining Association: Associated Lancashire Schools Examining Board, 12 Harter St, Manchester M1 6HL.

Southern Examining Group: Publications Dept, Stag Hill House, Guildford GU2 5XJ.

Welsh Joint Education Committee: Publications Dept, 245 Western Ave, Cardiff CF5 2YX.

Northern Ireland Schools Examinations Council: Publications Dept, Beechill House, 42 Beechill Rd, Belfast BT8 4RS.

One of the stated aims of the GCSE Music examination is 'to develop sensitivity towards music through personal experience by the exercise of imagination and the acquisition of skills and knowledge'. The examination itself is in three parts: *Listening, Performing* and *Composing*.

LISTENING
A written paper requires the candidate to respond to recorded music, both unprepared and prepared. For example, the candidate listens to a recorded passage and has to answer in one word:

'One of the instruments playing a long holding note below the melody is a _____.'

The great attraction of this examination is its flexibility. It offers many multiple-choice tests which you can answer at your own level.

PERFORMING
You can choose from the following options: any two out of three:

sing or play individually music previously prepared;
sing or play in ensemble music previously prepared;
rehearse and direct an ensemble.

any two out of three:

perform previously unseen music;
repeat musical phrases given aurally;
improvise.

COMPOSING
This is a coursework activity and includes arranging, improvising, melody writing and synthesizing, apart from actual composing, at the student's choice. Composing, as the official guide (*National Criteria: Music*) regards it, is 'the creation and organization of sound based on stimuli chosen either by the pupil or by the teacher'. The work submitted will be assessed by the candidate's teacher, 'subject to effective moderation, or by an external assessor'.

Students, teachers, parents and employers will want to know how GCSE results relate to the former GCE and CSE grades:

GCSE	GCE 'O' Level	CSE
A	A	
B	B	
C	C	Grade 1
D	C	Grade 2
E	D	Grade 3
F	E	Grade 4
G	Uncertificated	Grade 5
Ungraded	Uncertificated	Ungraded

New examination requirements are apt to provoke a chain reaction: candidates must be equipped with fresh skills and insights, and someone will have to provide the wherewithal. We are likely to see the following developments:

- Private instrumental and singing teachers will be in even greater demand than hitherto, in consequence of the GCSE *Performing* requirements. This will compensate for a probable drop in candidates taking Grade 5 examinations with a view to gaining exemption from certain sections of the former GCE. No such exemptions apply to GCSE.

- The comprehensive requirements for *Listening, Performing* and *Composing* necessitate a fresh approach in the classroom, with a consequent rise of the teacher's status.

- Visiting instrumental teachers who see their pupils largely out of school hours and therefore have scant links with school activities are going to be solicited to help a far greater number of pupils in their preparations for *Performing*. This will in turn enhance their prestige.

- A whole battery of textbooks and other teaching aids has already been created, and never before has the music profession been able to call on such brilliant material as:

Davies: *Beginning to Compose* (OUP)
GCSE: *An Approach to Composition* (cassette) (Hattrick)*

---

* Hattrick Music Services, 33 Goodmayes Lane, Ilford, Essex IG3 9PB.

James Ching Study Packs 1 to 5 (32 Cleveland Rd, London E18 2AL)
Middle Eight Music Kits (Middle Eight)
Paynter: *All Kinds of Music* (OUP)
Paynter: *Hear And Now* (Universal)
Salaman: *Listening In* (Pupils' and Teachers' Books with Cassettes) (Cramer)
Webb & Drewe: *Let's Make Music* (Teacher's Pack includes Books 1 to 5 and Answer Book) (Novello)

Detailed information about GCSE Music in:

GCSE *The National Criteria: Music* (HMSO)

- In the classroom, we can anticipate a renaissance of the Recorder, since even less gifted pupils may turn to this instrument for the *Performing* section.

- Since group activities are eligible for *Performing*, private teachers may well find an increased demand for such graded examinations as AB and T Piano Duet, T Guitar Duet, and T Ensembles.

- Accompanying a soloist or a group is another of the *Performing* options, and we may expect an all-round improvement in the skill and status of the accompanist.

- GCSE candidates are expected to be familiar with a wide range of musical styles, including jazz, pop and ethnic music. Clearly, teachers will vary in their familiarity with certain sections of the whole spectrum, and it may be desirable to combine classes of several schools, utilizing special talents of teachers in the district. Again, the prestige of those with specialist skills will be enhanced.

The GCSE Music syllabus is going to create musical awareness and musical literacy in vast numbers of students who, until now, would not have considered Music as one of their examination subjects. This must be a good thing.

Fact File II

Instrument manufacturers and retailers

LONDON

Vincent Bach, Unit 23, Garrick Ind. Centre, Garrick Rd, London
NW9 6AQ (Tel. 01 202 3711)

Chas. E. Foote, 17 Golden Sq, London W1R 3AG (Tel. 01 437 1811)

Howarth, 31 Chiltern St, London W1M 1HG (Tel. 01 935 2407)

Lewington, 144 Shaftesbury Ave, London WC2H 8HN (Tel.
01 240 0584)

Paxman, 116 Long Acre, London WC2E 9PA (Tel. 01 240 3642)

Pro/Brass, 2 Highgate Rd, London NW5 1NR (Tel. 01 267 2544)

Ward & Winterbourn, 75 Alexandra Rd, London NW4 2RX
(Tel. 01 203 2678)

AVON

Duck Son & Pinker, Pulteney Bridge, Bath BA2 4AU (Tel.
0225 65975)

BEDFORDSHIRE

Luton Music Centre, 114 Leagrave Rd, Luton LU4 8HX (Tel.
0582 26826)

Webb Music, 6 Bridge St, Leighton Buzzard LU7 7AL (Tel.
0525 376622)

BERKSHIRE

Hickie & Hickie, 153 Friar St, Reading RG1 1HE (Tel. 0734 55771)

BUCKINGHAMSHIRE

Rosehill Instruments, 64 London End, Beaconsfield HP9 2JD
(Tel. 04946 71717)

CAMBRIDGESHIRE

Cambridge Music Shop, 1A All Saints Passage, Cambridge CB2 3LT
(Tel. 0223 351786)

CHESHIRE

Bookland Music Shop, 12 Bridge St, Chester CH1 1NQ (Tel.
0244 313281)

Dawsons Music, 65 Sankey St, Warrington WA1 1SU (Tel.
0925 32591)

CLEVELAND

Williams & Son, 25 Brus House, Thornaby, Stockton-on-Tees, TS17 9ET (Tel. 0642 769614)

CORNWALL

West Country Music, 2 Highshore House, New Bridge St, Truro TR1 2AA (Tel. 0872 78501)

CUMBRIA

Brooks Music Centre, 97 Duke St, Whitehaven CA28 7EH (Tel. 0946 2116)

DERBYSHIRE

Wisher, 77 Osmaston Rd, Derby (Tel. 0332 44842)

DEVON

London Music Shop, 154 Sidwell St, Exeter EX4 6RT (Tel. 0392 36258)

DORSET

Dorset Music, Trendle St, Sherborne DT9 3NT (Tel. 0935 816332)

DYFED

Swales Music Centre, 2 High St, Haverfordwest SA61 2DJ (Tel. 0437 2059)

ESSEX

Brentwood Music Centre, 2 Ingrave Rd, Brentwood CM15 8AT (Tel. 0277 221210)

GLAMORGAN

Gwent Music, 2 Wharton St, Cardiff (Tel. 0222 31606)

Wilks Music Stores, 32 St Helens Rd, Swansea SA1 4AY (Tel. 0792 55953)

GLOUCESTERSHIRE

Duck Son & Pinker, 52 Southgate St, Gloucester GL1 2DR (Tel. 0452 21061)

GREATER MANCHESTER

Barratts of Manchester, 72 Oxford St, Manchester M1 5NH (Tel. 061 236 4470)

Music Exchange, Unit 2, Ringway Trading Estate, Wythenshawe, Manchester M22 6LX (Tel. 061 436 5110)

Forsyth, 126 Deansgate, Manchester M3 2GR (Tel. 061 834 3281)

GWENT

Gwent Music, 122 Commercial St, Newport (Tel. 0633 57505)

HAMPSHIRE

Whitwams Music, 70 High St, Winchester SO23 9DE (Tel. 0962 65253)

HERTFORDSHIRE

John Myatt, 55 Nightingale Rd, Hitchin SG5 1RE (Tel. 0462 35464)

HUMBERSIDE
Stevens Music, 97 Park St, Cleethorpes DN35 7LZ (Tel.
  0472 352293)
KENT
Billington, 172 Park View Rd, Welling DA16 1SU (Tel. 01 303 1429)
Fletcher Coppock & Newman, Morley Rd, Tonbridge TN9 1RA (Tel.
  0732 366421)
Forwoods Classical Music, 35 Palace St, Canterbury CT1 2DZ (Tel.
  0227 464741)
LANCASHIRE
Farfisa, Fraser St, Burnley BB10 1XJ (Tel. 0282 35431)
Music Box, 16 Whalley Rd, Accrington BB5 1AA (Tel. 0254 383571)
LEICESTERSHIRE
Abbey Studios, 312A Abbey Lane, Leicester (Tel. 0533 682051)
Premier Percussion, Blaby Rd, Wigston LE8 2DF (Tel. 0533 773121)
LINCOLNSHIRE
St Martins Music Shop, 13 Garmston St, Lincoln LN2 1HZ (Tel.
  0522 41839)
MERSEYSIDE
Crease, 14 County Rd, Liverpool L4 3QH (Tel. 051 525 3238)
Violin Family, 2A Maryland St, Liverpool L1 (Tel. 051 708 9575)
MIDDLESEX
Boosey & Hawkes, Deansbrook Rd, Edgware HA8 9BB (Tel.
  01 952 7711)
NORFOLK
Gibson Music, 75 St Augustine's St, Norwich NR3 3BG (Tel.
  0603 663262)
NORTHAMPTONSHIRE
Oundle Music, 13 West St, Oundle PE8 4EJ (Tel. 0832 73669)
NOTTINGHAMSHIRE
Windblowers, 75 Derby Rd, Nottingham NG1 5BA (Tel.
  0602 410543)
OXFORDSHIRE
Blackwells Music Shop, 38 Holywell St, Oxford OX1 3SW (Tel.
  0865 792792)
Holmes Music, 268 Banbury Rd, Summertown, Oxford OX2 7DY
  (Tel. 0865 57923)
SHROPSHIRE
Hilliard & Purslow, 17 Belle Vue Rd, Shrewsbury SY3 7LN (Tel.
  0743 56510)
SOMERSET
The Music Bar, 169 High St, Street BA16 0ND (Tel. 0458 45636)

STAFFORDSHIRE
Forsyth, 18 High St, Newcastle ST5 1RA (Tel. 0782 634041)
SUFFOLK
Galleon Music, High St, Aldeburgh IP15 5AX (Tel. 072885 3298)
SURREY
Dolmetsch Musical Instruments, 107 Blackdown Rural Industries,
    Haste Hill, Haslemere GU27 3AY (Tel. 0428 3235)
Stentor Music, Blackborough Rd, Reigate RH2 7EZ (Tel. 0737 240226)
SUSSEX
Music Supplies, 33 Warwick St, Worthing (Tel. 0903 208692)
Seaford Music, 24 Pevensey Rd, Eastbourne BN21 3HP (Tel.
    0323 32553)
TYNE AND WEAR
Williams, Earl Grey House, 23 Market St, Newcastle upon Tyne NE1
    6JE (Tel. 091 261 7641)
WARWICKSHIRE
Renton, High St, Leamington CV31 1LS (Tel. 0926 26703)
WILTSHIRE
Duck Son & Pinker, 59 Bridge St, Swindon SN1 1DP (Tel.
    0793 22018)
YORKSHIRE
Banks, 18 Lendal, York YO1 2AU (Tel. 0904 58836)
Dodds of Doncaster, 55 Christ Church Rd, Doncaster (Tel.
    0302 66008)
Forsyth, St George House, St George St, Leeds LS1 3DL (Tel.
    0532 444494)
Wood, 11 Market St, Huddersfield (Tel. 0484 27455)
SCOTLAND
Band Supplies, 5 Old Dumbarton Rd, Glasgow G3 8QY (Tel.
    041 339 9400)
Bruce Millers, 363 Union St, Aberdeen (Tel. 0224 59211)
Hay, 29 Friars St, Stirling FK8 1HE (Tel. 0786 73573)
Mackintosh Music, 6 Queensferry St, Edinburgh EH2 4PA (Tel.
    031 225 1171)
Music Shop, 29 Queensgate, Inverness IV1 1PQ (Tel. 0463 233374)
NORTHERN IRELAND
Marcus Musical Instruments, 113 North St, Belfast BT1 IND (Tel.
    0232 322871)
Sperrin Music Centre, 12 Blackrock Rd, Dunamore, Cookstown, Co
    Tyrone (Tel. 06487 51302)
ISLE OF MAN
Music Box, 56 Strand St, Douglas (Tel. 0624 22540)

Fact File III

Teach yourself the Recorder

Seven families collaborated with the author in a recent experiment, designed to establish whether a revival of music in the home, based on the Recorder, is indeed feasible.

There were four members in each group. None of the adults had ever played a musical instrument before. Most of the children had been taught to play the Recorder at school, but only two of them correctly. One of the adults was partially sighted, and one boy had respiratory problems (both took to the Recorder with ease). The purpose of the exercise was to see whether small family groups could be taught, in a short time, to play and enjoy the Recorder and whether they would continue playing together. The age range was five (youngest daughter) to seventy-four (grandfather). This was the procedure:

All groups were issued with wooden Descant Recorders and all were taught by the same method, as outlined further below. There were four sessions of just under an hour each. For the first five minutes everybody listened to a recording of a Vivaldi Recorder Sonata, played by Hans-Martin Linde (Deutsche Grammophon). This fine music, splendidly played, could not fail to inspire its listeners. The limpid, silvery sound produced by the soloist became everybody's model. The motto was *Inspiration – Imitation – Achievement*.

Next, each member of the group lit a candle. After taking a deep breath, they pursed their lips as for whistling, and directed a stream of air at the flame without extinguishing it. The aim was to cause the flame to bend sideways and to remain in that position for as long as possible, without significant flicker. By the end of the second session everybody had become an expert bender. The next project was to aim the air at the candlelight in such a way that it bent sideways as before, but was then slowly and steadily coaxed back into its upright position (*diminuendo*). The hardest task was left for the end – to direct a very small amount of air at the flame, then to increase it gradually, to cause it to bend over sideways without excessive flickering (*crescendo*). By the end of the fourth session everybody had achieved the set objectives and had thus absorbed some of the fundamentals of breath control, as a preliminary to correct tone production for the Recorder.

The next ten steps were taken, one after the other, in the course of the first or the first two tuition periods. The groups set out to learn a minimum of five notes, together with their musical notation. During the following sessions this range was extended to cover one and a half octaves. All students were encouraged to *tongue* their notes by breathing the syllable *too* into the mouthpiece, in order to achieve a clear *attack*. The following diagrams illustrate the procedure adopted for the first study session.

1 Grip the Recorder with your left hand. Play the note B:

   Both thumb and index finger are engaged. Whenever you want to hear this note, request it by calling 'BOTH!'

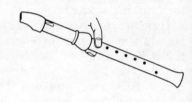

2 Play the note A:

   Another finger comes into play. Whenever you want to hear this note, request it by calling 'ANOTHER!'

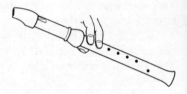

3 Play the note G:

   The ring finger is rather weak. It needs a good Grip to cover its hole successfully. Whenever you want to hear this note, request it by calling 'GRIP!'

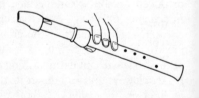

4 Play the note C:

   The middle, or Centre, finger alone is engaged. Whenever you want to hear this note, request it by calling 'CENTRE!'

5 Support the Recorder with your right hand. Play the note D:

Drop the thumb from the previous position. Whenever you want to hear this note, request it by calling 'DROP!'

6 and 7 Play all five notes:

Point at the required notes and practise them in any order.

Wipe out all small letters and repeat Step Six.

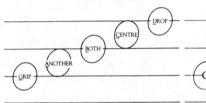 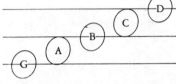

Associate the memory aids GRIP, ANOTHER, BOTH, CENTRE and DROP with the note names G, A, B, C and D.

8 Play and read all five notes, in any order, as requested:

Wipe out the Capitals and repeat Step Six. Also ask for the note names as you point them.

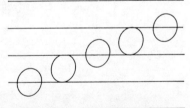

9 Play 'Oranges and lemons' from memory aids:

Teach 'Oranges and lemons' by calling:

Drop – Both – Drop – Both – Grip – Another – Both – Centre – Another – Drop – Both – Grip.

10 Play 'Oranges and lemons'
    from notation:
    Play without help.

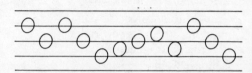

Using the same method, and restricting the present compass to the notes
G, A, B, C and D, the following songs were quickly mastered:

'Now the day is over'   'Hanschen klein'
'Winter adieu'   'Oh the grand old Duke of York'
'Little Bo-Peep'   'Sleep baby sleep'

The next Table lists individual results.

Time	How long until each player managed to play 'Oranges and lemons' faultlessly.
P	parent (or grandparent).
C	child.
Success rate	Did all members stay the course? Were they enthusiastic or did they have to be cajoled? Score out of ten.
Follow-up	All groups were revisited, seven to ten months later. Had they made further progress (+ or −), and were they still playing together (reg. = regularly, occ. = occasionally, nl = no longer)?

Group	Time (in minutes)	Success rate	Follow-up
A	P 42		
	P 38		
	C 35	9	+ reg.
	C 29		
B	P 67		
	P 59		
	C 63	5	− nl
	C 55		

Group	Time (in minutes)	Success rate	Follow-up
C	P 44 P 49 C 30 C 28	10	+ reg.
D	P 51 P 66 C 43 C 45	7	+ occ.
E	P 31 P 34 C 29 C 33	8	+ occ.
F	P 43 P 48 C 25 C 31	10	+ reg.
G	P 39 P 46 C 27 C 24	10	+ reg.

It must be conceded that the experiment was on a small scale, and that the tuition method was rough and ready, but there can be little doubt that families everywhere can learn to play and enjoy the Recorder quite rapidly. They can follow one of the established Tutors (see Suggested Study for the Recorder, p. 59). They can encourage and help each other. They can enlist additional players to join them. They can add to the Descant Recorder by taking up the Treble, Tenor and Bass (all share the same playing technique), forming a Recorder Consort, such as the Elizabethans would regard as one of the essentials of life. In short, the family can be greatly enriched and drawn together, once the Recorder is invited into the home.

Fact File IV

Music degrees and diplomas

ABCA	Associate of the British College of Accordionists
ABCM	Associate of the Bandsman's College of Music
ABSM	Associate of the Birmingham School of Music
ACCO	Associate of the Canadian College of Organists
A Cert. M	Archbishop of Canterbury's Diploma in Church Music
ACP	Associate of the College of Preceptors
ADCM	Archbishop of Canterbury's Diploma in Church Music
AGSM	Associate of the Guildhall School of Music and Drama
AKC	Associate of King's College, London
ALCM	Associate of the London College of Music
A Mus. A	Associate in Music, Australia
A Mus. LCM	Associate in General Musicianship of the London College of Music
A Mus. TCL	Associate in Compositional Technique of the Trinity College of Music
A Mus. TS	Associate in General Musicianship of the Tonic-Sol-Fa College of Music
ANSM	Associate of the Northern School of Music
ARAM	Associate of the Royal Academy of Music
ARCM	Associate of the Royal College of Music
ARCO	Associate of the Royal College of Organists
ARCO(CHM)	Associate of the Royal College of Organists, Choirmaster's Diploma
ARCT	Associate of the Toronto Royal Conservatory of Music
ARMCM	Associate of the Royal Manchester College of Music
ARNCM	Associate of the Royal Northern College of Music
ARSCM	Associate of the Royal School of Church Music
ATCL	Associate of the Trinity College of Music
ATSC	Associate of the Tonic-Sol-Fa College of Music
AUA	Associate Diploma in Music, Adelaide
BA	Bachelor of Arts
B Ed.	Bachelor of Education

B Hum.	Bachelor of Humanities
B Mus.	Bachelor of Music
B Phil.	Bachelor of Philosophy
CHM	Choirmaster's Diploma
Dip. Ed.	Diploma in Education
Dip. Mus. Ed.	Diploma in Musical Education
Dip. Mus. Ed. (RSAM)	Diploma in Musical Education, Royal Scottish Academy of Music and Drama
Dip. RAM	Recital Diploma of the Royal Academy of Music
Dip. T Mus.	Scottish Music Teaching Diploma
D Mus.	Doctor of Music
D Mus. (Cantuar)	Doctor of Music, awarded by the Archbishop of Canterbury
D Phil.	Doctor of Philosophy
DPLM	Diploma of Proficiency in Light Music, Leeds College of Music
DRSAM	Diploma in Music, Royal Scottish Academy of Music and Drama
DSCM	Diploma of the Sidney Conservatorium of Music
FACE	Fellow of the Australian College of Education
FAGO	Fellow of the American Guild of Organists
FBSM	Fellow of the Birmingham School of Music
FCCO	Fellow of the Canadian College of Organists
FCP	Fellow of the College of Preceptors
FGSM	Fellow of the Guildhall School of Music and Drama
FLCM	Fellow of the London College of Music
FNSM	Fellow of the Northern School of Music
FRAM	Fellow of the Royal Academy of Music
FRCM	Fellow of the Royal College of Music
FRCO	Fellow of the Royal College of Organists
FRCO(CHM)	Fellow of the Royal College of Organists, Choirmaster's Diploma
FRMCM	Fellow of the Royal Manchester College of Music
FRNCM	Fellow of the Royal Northern College of Music
FRSAM	Fellow of the Royal Scottish Academy of Music and Drama
FRSCM	Fellow of the Royal School of Church Music
FTCL	Fellow of the Trinity College of Music
FTSC	Fellow of the Tonic-Sol-Fa College of Music
FWCC	Fellow of Westminster Choir College, Princeton, USA
GBSM	Graduate of the Birmingham School of Music

GCLCM	Graduate of the Leeds College of Music
GDBM(SCT)	Graduate Diploma in Band Musicianship, Salford College of Technology
GGSM	Graduate of the Guildhall School of Music and Drama
GLCM	Graduate of the London College of Music
GNSM	Graduate of the Northern School of Music
GRNCM	Graduate of the Royal Northern College of Music
GRSM	Graduate of the Royal Schools of Music
GTCL	Graduate of the Trinity College of Music
Hon. ARAM	Honorary Associate of the Royal Academy of Music
Hon. ARCM	Honorary Associate of the Royal College of Music
Hon. FGSM	Honorary Fellow of the Guildhall School of Music and Drama
Hon. FRAM	Honorary Fellow of the Royal Academy of Music
Hon. FTCL	Honorary Fellow of the Trinity College of Music
Hon. FTSC	Honorary Fellow of the Tonic-Sol-Fa College of Music
Hon. GSM	Honorary Member of the Guildhall School of Music and Drama
Hon. LCM	Honorary Member of the London College of Music
Hon. RAM	Honorary Member of the Royal Academy of Music
Hon. RCM	Honorary Member of the Royal College of Music
Hon. RSCM	Honorary Member of the Royal School of Church Music
Hon. TSC	Honorary Member of the Tonic-Sol-Fa College of Music
LBCA	Licenciate of the British College of Accordionists
LBCM	Licenciate of the Bandsman's College of Music
LCP	Licenciate of the College of Preceptors
LGSM	Licenciate of the Guildhall School of Music and Drama
LISM	Licenciate of the Incorporated Society of Musicians
LLCM	Licenciate of the London College of Music
LMM	Licenciate of the Manitoba School of Music
L Mus. A	Licenciate in Music, Australia
L Mus. LCM	Licenciate in General Musicianship, London College of Music
L Mus. TCL	Licenciate in Compositional Techniques, Trinity College of Music
L Mus. TSC	Licenciate in General Musicianship, Tonic-Sol-Fa College of Music
LRAM	Licenciate of the Royal Academy of Music
LRSM	Licenciate of the Royal Schools of Music

LTCL	Licenciate of the Trinity College of Music
LTCL (GMT)	Licenciate in General Musicianship (Teachers), Trinity College of Music
LTCM	Licenciate of the Toronto Conservatory of Music
LTSC	Licenciate of the Tonic-Sol-Fa College of Music
LUCT	Licenciate of the University of Cape Town
LWCMD	Licenciate of the Welsh College of Music and Drama
MCP	Master of the College of Preceptors
MES	Member of the Music in Education Section, Incorporated Society of Musicians
MRST	Member of the Royal Society of Teachers
PPRNCM	Professional Performer of the Royal Northern College of Music
PTS	Member of the Private Teachers' Section, Incorporated Society of Musicians
RULM	Rhodes University Licenciate Diploma in Music
SPS	Member of the Solo Performers' Section, Incorporated Society of Musicians
UPLM	University of South Africa Performers Licenciate in Music

Fact File V

Locating teachers: telephone enquiries

Key to Abbreviations

CMA	County Music Adviser		S	Secretary
FE	College of Further Education		SSM	School specializing in Music
HM	Head of Music		TT	Teacher Training Establishment
MA	Music Adviser		U	University
MC	Music Colleges		YO	Youth Orchestra

Town	Who or what	Contact	Telephone	Town	Who or what	Contact	Telephone
Aberdeen	FE	HM	0224 572811	Birmingham	MA	MA	021 235 2570
	TT	HM	0224 482341		FE	HM	021 440 4288
	U	HM	0224 40241		FE	HM	021 476 8211
Aberystwyth	CMA	CMA	0970 617581		MC	S	021 359 6721
	U	HM	0970 4441		U	HM	021 472 1301
Accrington	FE	HM	0254 39352	Bishop			
Aldeburgh	YO	S	072885 2935	Auckland	CMA	CMA	0388 663665
Alton	FE	HM	0420 88118	Bolton	MA	MA	0204 22311
Andover	FE	HM	0264 63311	Boston	FE	HM	0205 68961
Ashton-				Bournemouth	CMA	CMA	0202 22151
under-Lyne	MA	MA	061330 8355	Bradford	MA	MA	0274 752588
Aylesbury	CMA	CMA	0296 5000		FE	HM	0274 753212
	FE	HM	0296 34111	Brent	MA	MA	01 903 1400
Ayr	CMA	CMA	0292 260325	Bridgend	CMA	CMA	0656 62111
Ballymena	CMA	CMA	0266 3333	Brighton	YO	S	0273 606622
Ballynahinch	CMA	CMA	0238 562030		U	HM	0273 606755
Bangor	TT	HM	0248 370171	Bristol	CMA	CMA	0272 290777
	U	HM	0248 351151		YO	S	0272 650036
Barking	MA	MA	01 594 7002		U	HM	0272 303030
Barnet	TT	HM	01 440 5181	Bromley	MA	MA	01 464 3333
Barnsley	MA	MA	0226 87621		MC	S	01 466 5092
Barnstaple	FE	HM	0271 45291	Bromsgrove	FE	HM	0527 79500
Basingstoke	FE	HM	0256 20861	Bury	MA	MA	061 761 512
Bath	TT	HM	02217 3701	Caernarfon	CMA	CMA	0286 4121
Bedford	CMA	CMA	0234 63222	Calderdale	MA	MA	0422 66456
	FE	HM	0234 42605	Cambridge	YO	S	0223 359340
Belfast	CMA	CMA	0232 229211		FE	HM	0223 63271
	TT	HM	0232 227678		U	HM	0223 61661
	TT	HM	0232 665271	Canterbury	TT	HM	0227 65548
	U	HM	0232 245133	Cardiff	CMA	CMA	0222 44291
Beverley	CMA	CMA	0482 861251		YO	S	0222 394711
Billingham	FE	HM	0642 552101		YO	S	0222 56123

Town	Who or what	Contact	Telephone	Town	Who or what	Contact	Telephone
Cardiff –	TT	HM	0222 55111	Enfield	MA	MA	01 366 9336
cont.	TT	HM	0222 42854		YO	S	01 363 2307
	MC	S	0222 42854	Epsom	YO	S	01 393 0873
	U	HM	0222 874816	Ewell	FE	HM	01 394 1731
Carlisle	CMA	CMA	0228 23456	Exeter	CMA	CMA	039287 6130
Carmarthen	CMA	CMA	0267 233333		FE	HM	0392 77977
	TT	HM	0267 237971		TT	HM	0392 263263
Chelmsford	CMA	CMA	0245 267222		U	HM	0392 77911
Chester	CMA	CMA	0244 603350	Exmouth	TT	HM	0395 265344
	FE	HM	0244 377595	Felixstowe	YO	S	0394 278161
	TT	HM	0244 375444	Forfar	CMA	CMA	0307 64413
Chichester	CMA	CMA	0243 777797	Gateshead	MA	MA	0632 783031
	FE	HM	0243 786321	Glasgow	CMA	CMA	041 227 2640
	TT	HM	0243 787911		YO	S	041 332 8311
Clwyd	CMA	CMA	0352 2121		FE	HM	041 649 4991
Colchester	YO	S	0206 28356		TT	HM	041 959 1232
	FE	HM	0206 570271		TT	HM	041 332 4101
Coventry	MA	MA	0203 418868		TT	HM	041 943 1424
Crewe	FE	HM	0270 69133		MC	S	041 332 4101
	TT	HM	09363 3231		U	HM	041 339 8855
Croydon	MA	MA	01 688 4433	Gloucester	CMA	CMA	0452 425448
Cwmbran	CMA	CMA	06333 67711	Grays	FE	HM	0375 371621
Dagenham	MA	MA	01 594 7002	Guildford	FE	HM	0483 31251
Dartington	FE	HM	0803 862224		U	HM	0483 571281
Derby	TT	HM	0332 514911	Hamilton	CMA	CMA	0698 282020
Dingwall	CMA	CMA	0349 63441	Harpenden	YO	S	05827 60014
Doncaster	MA	MA	0302 323556	Harrogate	FE	HM	0423 55631
Douglas				Harrow	MA	MA	01 863 5611
(IOM)	CMA	CMA	0624 27838		SSM	HM	01 422 1284
Dudley	MA	MA	0384 55433		YO	S	01 866 7481
Dumbarton	CMA	CMA	0389 65151		YO	S	01 863 2717
Dumfries	CMA	CMA	0387 69196		MC	S	01 427 2760
Dundee	CMA	CMA	0382 23281	Havant	FE	HM	07014 257011
	TT	HM	0382 453433	Havering	MA	MA	0708 66999
Dunoon	CMA	CMA	0369 6548	Hemel			
Durham	FE	HM	0385 62421	Hempstead	FE	HM	0442 63771
	TT	HM	0385 245931	Hereford	FE	HM	0432 265725
	U	HM	0385 64466	Hertford	CMA	CMA	0992 555951
Edinburgh	CMA	CMA	031 343 1931	High			
	SSM	HM	031 332 7805	Wycombe	FE	HM	0492 22141
	SSM	HM	031 225 1831	Hillingdon	MA	MA	0895 50457
	YO	S	031 334 4802	Hinckley	FE	HM	0455 632388
	YO	S	031 667 7462	Hitchin	FE	HM	0462 32351
	YO	S	031 225 7592	Hounslow	MA	MA	01 568 4601
	FE	HM	031 444 2266	Huddersfield	FE	HM	0484 536521
	FE	HM	031 453 6161	Hull	CMA	CMA	0482 223151
	TT	HM	031 556 8455		YO	S	0482 650493
	U	HM	031 667 1011		U	HM	0482 46311
Egham	U	HM	07843 34455	Huntingdon	CMA	CMA	0480 52181
Elgin	CMA	CMA	0343 41144		YO	S	0480 69832

191

Town	Who or what	Contact	Telephone
Huntingdon – cont.	FE	HM	0480 52346
Ipswich	CMA	CMA	0473 52846
Keele	U	HM	0782 621111
Kidderminster	FE	HM	0562 820811
Kings Lynn	FE	HM	0553 761144
Kingston upon Thames	MA	MA	01 546 2121
	CMA	CMA	01 541 9481
	TT	HM	01 549 1141
Kirklees	MA	MA	0484 537399
Kirkwall	CMA	CMA	0856 3535
Knowsley	MA	MA	051 480 5111
Lancaster	FE	HM	0524 66215
	TT	HM	0524 63446
	U	HM	0524 65201
Leeds	MA	MA	0532 463882
	FE	HM	0532 452069
	TT	HM	0532 759061
	U	HM	0532 431751
Leicester	CMA	CMA	0533 551378
	FE	HM	0533 551378
	U	HM	0533 522781
Lerwick	CMA	CMA	0595 3535
Lewes	CMA	CMA	07916 472336
	FE	HM	0273 476121
Leyland	FE	HM	07744 32511
Lincoln	CMA	CMA	0522 29931
	TT	HM	0522 27347
Liverpool	MA	MA	051 236 5480
	YO	S	051 709 2895
	FE	HM	051 733 5511
	TT	HM	051 722 7331
	U	HM	051 709 6022
Llandrindod Wells	CMA	CMA	0597 3711
London E17	MA	MA	01 521 2021
London EC1	U	HM	01 253 4399
London EC2	MC	S	01 628 2571
London N1	YO	S	01 251 6472
London N11	MA	MA	01 368 1255
London N14	FE	HM	01 886 6521
London N22	MA	MA	01 881 3000
London NW1	FE	HM	01 387 2037
	MC	S	01 935 5461
London NW10	MC	S	01 451 0376
London SE1	FE	HM	01 928 9561
	MC	S	01 261 9267
London SE3	MC	S	01 952 0234
London SE4	FE	HM	01 692 0353
London SE8	YO	S	01 691 5418
	MC	S	01 691 0307
London SE9	TT	HM	01 850 0081
London SE14	YO	S	01 692 7171
	MC	S	01 692 9291
	U	HM	01 692 7171
London SW1	SSM	HM	01 828 0881
	YO	S	01 235 6641
London SW7	MC	S	01 589 3643
London SW19	TT	HM	01 946 2234
London W1	MC	S	01 437 6120
	MC	S	01 935 5773
London W5	MA	MA	01 579 2424
	YO	S	01 993 3135
	FE	HM	01 579 4111
London WC1	FE	HM	01 837 8185
London WC2	U	HM	01 836 5454
Lymington	FE	HM	0590 23565
Maidstone	CMA	CMA	0622 690404
Manchester	MA	MA	061 273 3630
	SSM	HM	061 834 9644
	TT	HM	061 445 7871
	MC	S	061 273 6283
	U	HM	061 273 3356
Markinch (Fife)	CMA	CMA	0592 756633
Matlock	CMA	CMA	0629 3411
Merton	MA	MA	01 545 3305
Middlesbrough	CMA	CMA	0642 248155
Milton Keynes	U	HM	0908 74066
Nelson	FE	HM	0282 603151
Newark	FE	HM	0636 705921
Newcastle upon Tyne	MA	MA	091 274 3620
	FE	HM	091 273 8866
	U	HM	091 232 8511
Newport (Gwent)	FE	HM	0495 270295
	TT	HM	0633 421292
Newport (IOW)	CMA	CMA	0983 524031
Newtownabbey	U	HM	0232 365131
Newtown St Boswells	CMA	CMA	0835 23301
Northallerton	CMA	CMA	0609 3123
Northampton	CMA	CMA	0604 37117

Town	Who or what	Contact	Telephone	Town	Who or what	Contact	Telephone
Northampton –				Scarborough	TT	HM	0723 362392
cont.	TT	HM	0604 715000	Scunthorpe	CMA	CMA	0742 856101
North					FE	HM	0742 855022
Shields	MA	MA	091 258 0848	Sefton	MA	MA	07048 72773
Norwich	CMA	CMA	0603 611122	Sevenoaks	YO	S	073275 344
	FE	HM	0603 60011	Sheffield	MA	MA	0742 735193
	U	HM	0603 56161		U	HM	0742 667234
Nottingham	CMA	CMA	0602 860232	Shrewsbury	CMA	CMA	0743 254507
	FE	HM	0602 607201	Solihull	MA	MA	021 704 6619
	U	HM	0602 506101	.	FE	HM	021 705 6376
Nuneaton	FE	HM	0203 349321	Southampton	TT	HM	0703 228761
Oldham	MA	MA	061 624 6831		U	HM	0703 559122
Omagh	CMA	CMA	0662 42083	Southport	YO	S	0704 30601
Ormskirk	TT	HM	0695 75171	South Shields	MA	MA	091 454 0431
Oswestry	FE	HM	0691 653067	Stafford	CMA	CMA	0785 3121
Oxford	CMA	CMA	0865 815234	Stirling	CMA	CMA	0786 73111
	YO	S	0865 862877		U	HM	0786 73171
	TT	HM	08677 2691	Stoke	FE	HM	0782 202561
	U	HM	0865 276125	Stoke			
Paisley	CMA	CMA	041 889 5454	d'Abernon	SSM	HM	0932 64739
Perth	CMA	CMA	0738 38101	Stornoway	CMA	CMA	0851 3773
Peterborough	FE	HM	0733 67366	Stratford-			
Pontypool	FE	HM	0495 55141	upon-Avon	FE	HM	0789 66245
Poole	FE	HM	0202 747600	Street	FE	HM	0458 42277
Portadown	CMA	CMA	0762 38321	Sunderland	MA	MA	091 514 1311
Preston	CMA	CMA	0772 54868		TT	HM	0783 76231
	YO	S	0772 717787	Sutton	MA	MA	01 661 5713
	FE	HM	0772 716511	Swansea	CMA	CMA	0792 471374
Reading	CMA	CMA	0734 665015	Swindon	CMA	CMA	0793 33531
	TT	HM	0734 663387		FE	HM	0793 40131
	U	HM	0734 873583	Taunton	CMA	CMA	0823 73451
Redbridge	MA	MA	01 501 3945	Tonbridge	FE	HM	0732 358101
Redcar	FE	HM	0642 473132	Torquay	FE	HM	0803 217619
Redruth	FE	HM	0209 715829	Truro	CMA	CMA	0872 74282
Richmond				Twickenham	FE	HM	01 892 6656
upon Thames	MA	MA	01 891 1411		FE	HM	01 891 0121
Rochdale	MA	MA	0706 521100	Wakefield	MA	MA	0924 370211
Romford	FE	HM	0708 66841		FE	HM	0924 370501
Rotherham	MA	MA	0709 2121		TT	HM	0924 85261
Rugby	FE	HM	0788 73133	Wallasey	FE	HM	051 639 8371
St Andrews	U	HM	0334 76161	Walsall	MA	MA	0922 491320
St Helens	MA	MA	0744 52930		TT	HM	0922 29141
St Peter Port				Warrington	YO	S	0925 65456
(Guernsey)	CMA	CMA	0481 710821	Warwick	CMA	CMA	0926 493431
St Saviour				Watford	FE	HM	0923 40311
(Jersey)	CMA	CMA	0534 71065	Wells	SSM	HM	0749 72117
Sale	MA	MA	061 973 2253	Wigan	MA	MA	0942 44991
Salford	MA	MA	061 832 9751		FE	HM	0942 608811
	FE	HM	061 834 6633	Winchester	CMA	CMA	0962 61502
Sandwell	MA	MA	021 525 7366		FE	HM	0962 52764

V LOCATING TEACHERS: TELEPHONE ENQUIRIES

Town	Who or what	Contact	Telephone	Town	Who or what	Contact	Telephone
Winchester –							
cont.	TT	HM	0962 62281	Worcester	CMA	CMA	0905 35336
Wirral	MA	MA	051 647 7000		TT	HM	0905 42808C
Wisbech	FE	HM	0945 582561	Yeovil	FE	HM	0935 23921
Wolver-				York	TT	HM	0904 56771
hampton	MA	MA	0902 27811		U	HM	0904 59861

Index